SCIENCE FUSION

Lab Manual

Module I

HOLT McDOUGAL

HOUGHTON MIFFLIN HARCOURT

Acknowledgements for Covers

Cover Photo Credits

Skier (bg) ©*David Stoecklein/Corbis; pacific wheel* (l) ©Geoffrey George/Getty Images; *snowboarder* (cl) ©Jonathan Nourok/Photographer's Choice/Getty Images; *water droplet* (cr) ©L. Clarke/Corbis; *molecular structure* (r) ©Stockbyte/Getty Images

Printed in the U.S.A.

ISBN 978-0-547-59261-9

3 4 5 6 7 8 9 10 0868 20 19 18 17 16 15 14 13 12 11
4500316664 A B C D E F G

Contents

INTRODUCTION

TEACHER LAB SAFETY

STUDENT LAB SAFETY

Unit 1 Motion and Forces

Unit 2 Work, Energy, and Machines

Unit 3 Electricity and Magnetism

Using Your *ScienceFusion* Lab Program

Your *ScienceFusion* Lab Program is designed to include activities that address a variety of student levels, inquiry levels, time availability, and materials. In this Lab Manual, you will find that each student activity is preceded by Teacher Resources with valuable information about the activity.

Activity Type: Quick Lab

Each lesson within each unit is supported by two to three short activities called Quick Labs. Quick Labs involve simple materials and set-up. The student portion of each Quick Lab should take less than 30 minutes. Each Quick Lab includes Teacher Resources and one Student Datasheet.

Activity Types: Exploration Lab, Field Lab, and S.T.E.M. Lab

Each unit is supported by one to four additional labs that require one or more class periods to complete. Each Exploration, Field, and S.T.E.M. Lab includes Teacher Resources and two Student Datasheets. Each Student Datasheet is targeted to address different inquiry levels. Below is a description of each lab:

- **Exploration Labs** are traditional lab activities. The labs are designed to be conducted with standard laboratory equipment and materials.
- **Field Labs** are lab activities that are partially or completely performed outside the classroom or laboratory.
- **S.T.E.M. Labs** are lab activities that focus on Science, Technology, Engineering, and Math skills.

Inquiry Level

The inquiry level of each activity indicates the level at which students direct the activity. An activity that is entirely student-directed is often called Open Inquiry or Independent Inquiry. True Open or Independent Inquiry is based on a question posed by students, uses experimental processes designed by students, and requires students to find the connections between data and content. These types of activities result from student interest in the world around them. The *ScienceFusion* Lab Program provides activities that allow for a wide variety of student involvement.

- DIRECTED Inquiry is the least student-directed of the inquiry levels. Directed Inquiry activities provide students with an introduction to content, a procedure to follow, and direction on how to organize and analyze data.
- GUIDED Inquiry indicates that an activity is moderately student-directed. Guided Inquiry activities require students to select materials, procedural steps, data analysis techniques, or other aspects of the activity.
- INDEPENDENT Inquiry indicates that an activity is highly student-directed. Though students are provided with ideas, partial procedures, or suggestions, they are responsible for selecting many aspects of the activity.

Each Quick Lab includes one Student Datasheet that is written to support the inquiry level indicated on the Teacher Resources. Each Exploration Lab, Field Lab, and S.T.E.M. Lab includes two Student Datasheets, each written to support an inquiry level. In addition, the Teacher Resources includes one or more modification suggestions to adjust the inquiry level.

Student Level

The *ScienceFusion* Lab Program is designed to provide successful experiences for all levels of students.

- BASIC activities focus on introductory content and concepts taught in the lesson. These activities can be used with any level of student, including those who may have learning or language difficulties, but they may not provide a challenge for advanced students.
- GENERAL activities are appropriate for most students.
- ADVANCED activities require good understanding of the content and concepts in the lesson or ask students to manipulate content to arrive at the learning objective. Advanced activities may provide a challenge to advanced students, but they may be difficult for average or basic-level students.

Lab Ratings

Each activity is rated on three criteria to provide you with information that you may find useful when determining if an activity is appropriate for your resources.

- **Teacher Prep** rating indicates the amount of preparation you will need to provide before students can perform the activity.
- **Student Setup** rating indicates the amount of preparation students will need to perform before they begin to collect data.
- **Cleanup** rating indicates the amount of effort required to dispose of materials and disassemble the set-up of the activity.

Teacher Notes

Information and background that may be helpful to you can be found in the Teacher Notes section of the Teacher Resources. The information includes hints and a list of skills that students will practice during the activity.

Science Kit

Hands-on materials needed to complete all the labs in the Lab Manual for each module have been conveniently configured into consumable and non-consumable kits. Common materials provided by parents or your school/district are not included in the kits. Laboratory equipment commonly found in most schools has been separately packaged in a Grades 6–8 Inquiry Equipment Kit. This economical option allows schools to buy equipment only if they need it and can be shared among teachers and across grade levels. For more information on the material kits or to order, contact your local Holt McDougal sales representative or call customer service at 800-462-6595.

Online Lab Resources

The *ScienceFusion* Lab Program offers many additional resources online through our web site thinkcentral.com. These resources include:

Teacher Notes, Transparencies, and **Copymasters** are found in the Online Toolkit. Student-friendly tutorial Transparencies are available to print as transparencies or handouts. Each set of Transparencies is supported by Teacher Notes that include background information, teaching tips, and techniques. Teacher Notes, Transparencies, and Copymatsters are available to teach a broad range of skills.

- **Modeling Experimental Design** Teacher Notes and Transparencies cover Scientific Methods skills, such as Making Qualitative Observations, Developing a Hypothesis, and Making Valid Inferences.

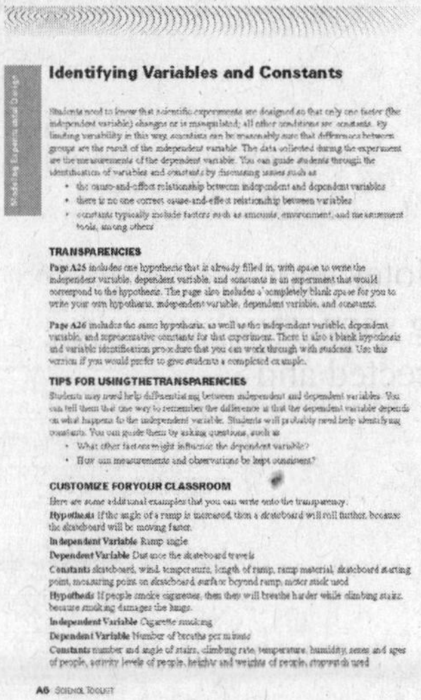

Identifying Variables and Constants

Students need to know that scientific experiments are designed so that only one factor (the independent variable) changes or is manipulated; all other conditions are constants. By limiting variability in this way, scientists can be reasonably sure that differences between groups are the result of the independent variable. The data collected during the experiment are the measurements of the dependent variable. You can guide students through the identification of variables and constants by discussing issues such as

- the cause-and-effect relationship between independent and dependent variables
- there is no one correct cause-and-effect relationship between variables
- constants typically include factors such as amounts, environment, and measurement tools, among others

TRANSPARENCIES

Page A25 includes one hypothesis that is already filled in, with space to write the independent variable, dependent variable, and constants in an experiment that would correspond to the hypothesis. The page also includes a completely blank space for you to write your own hypothesis, independent variable, dependent variable, and constants.

Page A26 includes the same hypothesis, as well as the independent variable, dependent variable, and representative constants for that experiment. There is also a blank hypothesis and variable identification procedure that you can work through with students. Use this version if you would prefer to give students a completed example.

TIPS FOR USING THE TRANSPARENCIES

Students may need help differentiating between independent and dependent variables. You can tell them that one way to remember the difference is that the dependent variable depends on what happens to the independent variable. Students will probably need help identifying constants. You can guide them by asking questions, such as

- What other factors might influence the dependent variable?
- How can measurements and observations be kept consistent?

CUSTOMIZE FOR YOUR CLASSROOM

Here are some additional examples that you can write onto the transparency.

Hypothesis If the angle of a ramp is increased, then a skateboard will roll farther, because the skateboard will be moving faster.

Independent Variable Ramp angle

Dependent Variable Distance the skateboard travels

Constants skateboard, wind, temperature, length of ramp, ramp material, skateboard starting point, measuring point on skateboard, surface beyond ramp, meter stick used

Hypothesis If people smoke cigarettes, then they will breathe harder while climbing stairs, because smoking damages the lungs.

Independent Variable Cigarette smoking

Dependent Variable Number of breaths per minute

Constants number and angle of stairs, climbing rate, temperature, humidity, sexes and ages of people, activity levels of people, heights and weights of people, stopwatch used

A6 Science Toolkit

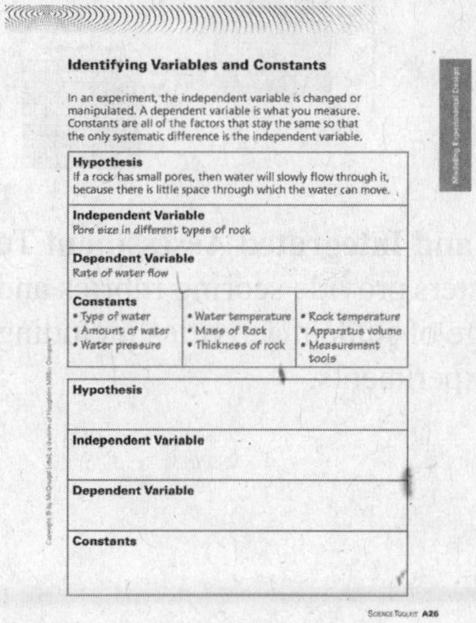

Identifying Variables and Constants

In an experiment, the independent variable is changed or manipulated. A dependent variable is what you measure. Constants are all of the factors that stay the same so that the only systematic difference is the independent variable.

Hypothesis If a rock has small pores, then water will slowly flow through it, because there is little space through which the water can move.		
Independent Variable Pore size in different types of rock		
Dependent Variable Rate of water flow		
Constants • Type of water • Amount of water • Water pressure	• Water temperature • Mass of Rock • Thickness of rock	• Rock temperature • Apparatus volume • Measurement tools

Hypothesis
Independent Variable
Dependent Variable
Constants

Science Toolkit A26

- **Writing in the Sciences** Teacher Notes and Transparencies teach written communication skills, such as Writing a Lab Report and Maintaining a Science Notebook. In addition, the Lab Report Template provides a structured format that students can use as the basis for their own lab reports.

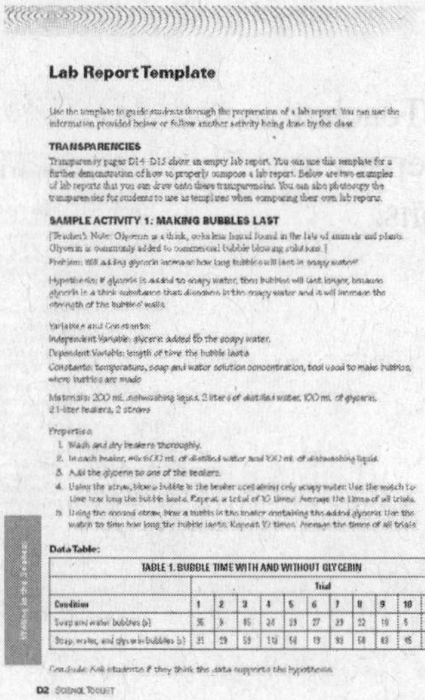

Lab Report Template

Use the template to guide students through the preparation of a lab report. You can use the information provided below or follow another activity being done by the class.

TRANSPARENCIES

Transparency pages D14–D15 show an empty lab report. You can use this template for a further demonstration of how to properly compose a lab report. Below are two examples of lab reports that you can draw onto these transparencies. You can also photocopy the transparencies for students to use as templates when composing their own lab reports.

SAMPLE ACTIVITY 1: MAKING BUBBLES LAST

[Teacher's Note: Glycerin is a thick, colorless liquid found in the fats of animals and plants. Glycerin is commonly added to commercial bubble blowing solutions.]

Problem: Will adding glycerin increase how long bubbles will last in soapy water?

Hypothesis: If glycerin is added to soapy water, then bubbles will last longer, because glycerin is a thick substance that dissolves in the soapy water and it will increase the strength of the bubbles' walls.

Variables and Constants:

Independent Variable: glycerin added to the soapy water

Dependent Variable: length of time the bubble lasts

Constants: temperature, soap and water solution concentration, tool used to make bubbles, where bubbles are made

Materials: 200 mL dishwashing liquid, 2 liters of distilled water, 100 mL of glycerin, 2 1-liter beakers, 2 straws

Procedure:

1. Wash and dry beakers thoroughly.
2. In each beaker, mix 600 mL of distilled water and 100 mL of dishwashing liquid.
3. Add the glycerin to one of the beakers.
4. Using the straw, blow a bubble in the beaker containing only soapy water. Use the watch to time how long the bubble lasts. Repeat a total of 10 times. Average the times of all trials.
5. Using the second straw, blow a bubble in the beaker containing the added glycerin. Use the watch to time how long the bubble lasts. Repeat 10 times. Average the times of all trials.

Data Table:

TABLE 1. BUBBLE TIME WITH AND WITHOUT GLYCERIN											
	Trial										
Condition	1	2	3	4	5	6	7	8	9	10	Mean
Soap and water bubbles (s)	36	9	[illegible]	24	[illegible]	27	[illegible]	22	19	5	[illegible]
Soap, water, and glycerin bubbles (s)	[illegible]	29	59	[illegible]	56	19	[illegible]	58	[illegible]	[illegible]	55

Conclude: Ask students if they think the data supports the hypothesis.

D2 Science Toolkit

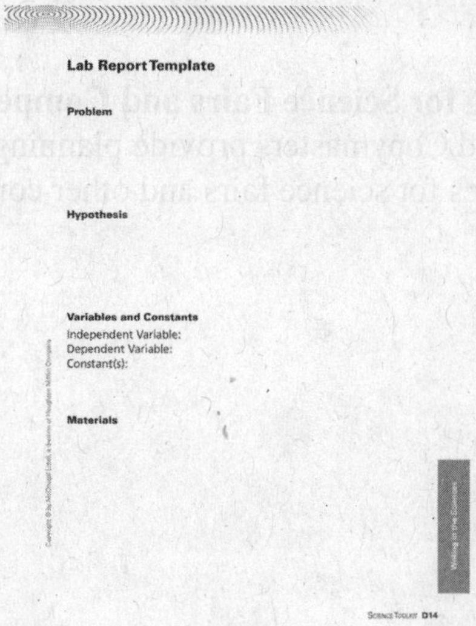

Lab Report Template

Problem

Hypothesis

Variables and Constants

Independent Variable:

Dependent Variable:

Constant(s):

Materials

Science Toolkit D14

- **Math in Science Tools** Teacher Notes and Transparencies teach the math skills that are needed for data analysis in labs. These Teacher Notes and Transparencies support the S.T.E.M. concepts found throughout the *ScienceFusion* program.

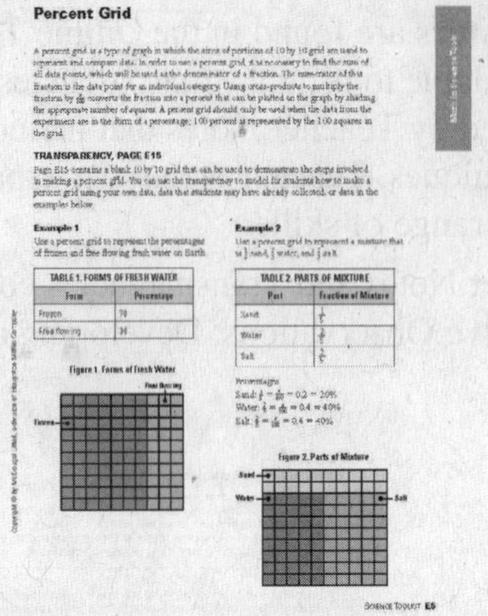

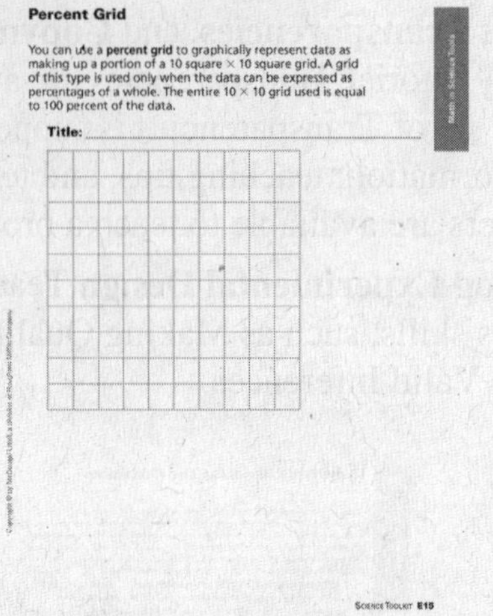

- **Rubrics and Integrated Assessment** Teacher Notes and Copymasters provide scoring rubrics and grading support for a range of student activities including self-directed and guided experiments.

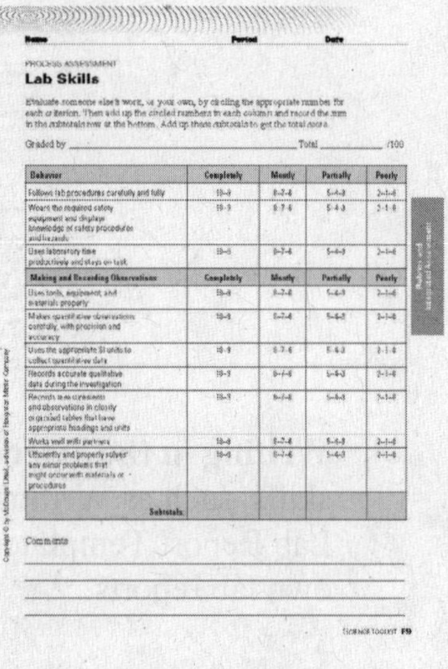

- **Planning for Science Fairs and Competitions** Teacher Notes and Copymasters provide planning and preparation techniques for science fairs and other competitions.

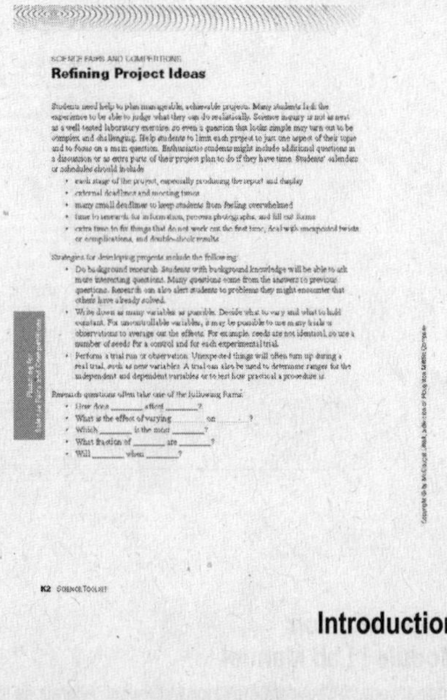

Making Your Laboratory a Safe Place

Concern for safety must begin before any activity in the classroom and before students enter the lab. A careful review of the facilities should be a basic part of preparation for each school term. You should investigate the physical environment, identify any safety risks, and inspect your work areas for compliance with safety regulations.

The review of the lab should be thorough, and all safety issues must be addressed immediately. Keep a file of your review, and add to the list each year. This will allow you to continue to raise the standard of safety in your lab and classroom.

Many classroom experiments, demonstrations, and other activities are classics that have been used for years. This familiarity may lead to a comfort that can obscure inherent safety concerns. Review all experiments, demonstrations, and activities for safety concerns before presenting them to the class. Identify and eliminate potential safety hazards.

1. **Identify the Risks** Before introducing any activity, demonstration, or experiment to the class, analyze it and consider what could possibly go wrong. Carefully review the list of materials to make sure they are safe. Inspect the equipment in your lab or classroom to make sure it is in good working order. Read the procedures to make sure they are safe. Record any hazards or concerns you identify.
2. **Evaluate the Risks** Minimize the risks you identified in the last step without sacrificing learning. Remember that no activity you perform in the lab or classroom is worth risking injury. Thus, extremely hazardous activities, or those that violate your school's policies, must be eliminated. For activities that present smaller risks, analyze each risk carefully to determine its likelihood. If the pedagogical value of the activity does not outweigh the risks, the activity must be eliminated.
3. **Select Controls to Address Risks** Even low-risk activities require controls to eliminate or minimize the risks. Make sure that in devising controls you do not substitute an equally or more hazardous alternative. Some control methods include the following:
   - Explicit verbal and written warnings may be added or posted.
   - Equipment may be rebuilt or relocated, parts may be replaced, or equipment be replaced entirely by safer alternatives.
   - Risky procedures may be eliminated.
   - Activities may be changed from student activities to teacher demonstrations.
4. **Implement and Review Selected Controls** Controls do not help if they are forgotten or not enforced. The implementation and review of controls should be as systematic and thorough as the initial analysis of safety concerns in the lab and laboratory activities.

Safety with Chemicals

Label student reagent containers with the substance's name and hazard class(es) (flammable, reactive, etc.). Dispose of hazardous waste chemicals according to federal, state, and local regulations. Refer to the MSDS for recommended disposal procedures. Remove all sources of flames, sparks, and heat from the laboratory when any flammable material is being used.

Material Safety Data Sheets

The purpose of a Material Safety Data Sheet (MSDS) is to provide readily accessible information on chemical substances commonly used in the science laboratory or in industry. The MSDS should be kept on file and referred to BEFORE handling ANY chemical. The MSDS can also be used to instruct students on chemical hazards, to evaluate spill and disposal procedures, and to warn of incompatibility with other chemicals or mixtures.

Storing Chemicals

Never store chemicals alphabetically, as this greatly increases the risk of promoting a violent reaction.

Storage Suggestions

1. Always lock the storeroom and all its cabinets when not in use.
2. Students should not be allowed in the storeroom and preparation area.
3. Avoid storing chemicals on the floor of the storeroom.
4. Do not store chemicals above eye level or on the top shelf in the storeroom.
5. Be sure shelf assemblies are firmly secured to the walls.
6. Provide anti-roll lips on all shelves.
7. Shelving should be constructed out of wood. Metal cabinets and shelves are easily corroded.
8. Avoid metal, adjustable shelf supports and clips. They can corrode, causing shelves to collapse.
9. Acids, flammables, poisons, and oxidizers should each be stored in their own locking storage cabinet.

Safety with Animals

It is recommended that teachers follow the NABT Position Statement "The Use of Animals in Biology Education" issued by the National Association of Biology Teachers (available at www.nabt.org).

Safety In Handling Preserved Materials

The following practices are recommended when handling preserved specimens:

1. NEVER dissect road-kills or nonpreserved slaughterhouse materials.
2. Wear protective gloves and splash-proof safety goggles at all times when handling preserving fluids and preserved specimens and during dissection.
3. Wear lab aprons. Use of an old shirt or smock under the lab apron is recommended.
4. Conduct dissection activities in a well-ventilated area.
5. Do not allow preservation or body-cavity fluids to contact skin. Fixatives do not distinguish between living or dead tissues. Biological supply firms may use formalin-based fixatives of varying concentrations to initially fix zoological and botanical specimens. Some provide specimens that are freezedried and rehydrated in a 10% isopropyl alcohol solution. Many suppliers provide fixed botanical materials in 50% glycerin.

Reduction Of Free Formaldehyde

Currently, federal regulations mandate a permissible exposure level of 0.75 ppm for formaldehyde. Contact your supplier for Material Data Safety Sheet (MSDS) that details the amount of formaldehyde present as well as gas-emitting characteristics for individual specimens. Prewash specimens (in a loosely covered container) in running tap water for 1–4 hours to dilute the fixative. Formaldehyde may also be chemically bound (thereby reducing danger) by immersing washed specimens in a 0.5–1.0% potassium bisulfate solution overnight or by placing them in 1% phenoxyethanol holding solutions.

Safety with Microbes

WHAT YOU CAN'T SEE CAN HURT YOU

Pathogenic (disease-causing) microorganisms are not appropriate investigation tools in the high school laboratory and should never be used.

Consult with the school nurse to screen students whose immune systems may be compromised by illness or who may be receiving immunosuppressive drug therapy. Such individuals are extraordinarily sensitive to potential infection from generally harmless microorganisms and should not participate in laboratory activities unless permitted to do so by a physician. Do not allow students who have any open cuts, abrasions, or open sores to work with microorganisms.

HOW TO USE ASEPTIC TECHNIQUE

- Demonstrate correct aseptic technique to students prior to conducting a lab activity. Never pipet liquid media by mouth. When possible, use sterile cotton applicator sticks instead of inoculating loops and Bunsen burner flames for culture inoculation. Remember to use appropriate precautions when disposing of cotton applicator sticks: they should be autoclaved or sterilized before disposal.
- Treat all microbes as pathogenic. Seal with tape all petri dishes containing bacterial cultures. Do not use blood agar plates, and never attempt to cultivate microbes from a human or animal source.
- Never dispose of microbe cultures without sterilizing them first. Autoclave or steam-sterilize at 120°C and 15 psi for 15 to 20 minutes all used cultures and any materials that have come in contact with them. If these devices are not available, flood or immerse these articles in full-strength household bleach for 30 minutes, and then discard. Use the autoclave or steam sterilizer yourself; do not allow students to use these devices.
- Wash all lab surfaces with a disinfectant solution before and after handling bacterial cultures.

HOW TO HANDLE BACTERIOLOGICAL SPILLS

- Never allow students to clean up bacteriological spills. Keep on hand a spill kit containing 500 mL of full-strength household bleach, biohazard bags (autoclavable), forceps, and paper towels.
- In the event of a bacterial spill, cover the area with a layer of paper towels. Wet the paper towels with bleach, and allow them to stand for 15 to 20 minutes. Wearing gloves and using forceps, place the residue in the biohazard bag. If broken glass is present, use a brush and dustpan to collect material, and place it in a suitably marked puncture-resistant container for disposal.

Personal Protective Equipment

Chemical goggles (Meeting ANSI Standard Z87.1) These should be worn with any chemical or chemical solution other than water, when heating substances, using any mechanical device, or observing physical processes that could eject an object.

Face shield (Meeting ANSI Standard Z87.1) Use in combination with eye goggles when working with corrosives.

Contact lenses The wearing of contact lenses for cosmetic reasons should be prohibited in the laboratory. If a student must wear contact lenses prescribed by a physician, that student should be instructed to wear eye-cup safety goggles, similar to swimmer's cup goggles, meeting ANSI Standard Z87.1.

Eye-wash station The device must be capable of delivering a copious, gentle flow of water to both eyes for at least 15 minutes. Portable liquid supply devices are not satisfactory and should not be used. A plumbed-in fixture or a perforated spray head on the end of a hose attached to a plumbed-in outlet is suitable if it is designed for use as an eye-wash fountain and meets ANSI Standard Z358.1. It must be within a 30-second walking distance from any spot in the room.

Safety shower (Meeting ANSI Standard Z358.1) Location should be within a 30-second walking distance from any spot in the room. Students should be instructed in the use of the safety shower in the event of a fire or chemical splash on their body that cannot simply be washed off.

Gloves Polyethylene, neoprene rubber, or disposable plastic may be used. Nitrile or butyl rubber gloves are recommended when handling corrosives.

Apron Rubber-coated cloth or vinyl (nylon-coated) halter is recommended.

Student Safety in the Laboratory

Systematic, careful lab work is an essential part of any science program. The equipment and apparatus students will use present various safety hazards. You must be aware of these hazards before students engage in any lab activity. The Teacher Resource Pages at the beginning of each lab in this Lab Manual will guide you in properly directing the equipment use during the experiments. Photocopy the information on the following pages for students. These safety rules always apply in the lab and in the field.

Name ______________________ Class ____________ Date ____________

Safety Symbols

The following safety symbols will appear in the instructions for labs and activities to emphasize important notes of caution. Learn what they represent so that you can take the appropriate precautions.

Eye Protection

- Wear approved safety goggles at all times in the lab as directed.
- If chemicals get into your eyes, flush your eyes immediately.
- Do not wear contact lenses in the lab.
- Do not look directly at the sun or any intense light source or laser.

Hand Safety

- Do not cut an object while holding the object in your hand.
- Wear appropriate protective gloves when working with an open flame, chemicals, solutions, or wild or unknown plants.
- Use a heat-resistant mitt to handle equipment that may be hot.

Clothing Protection

- Wear an apron or lab coat at all times in the lab.
- Tie back long hair, secure loose clothing, and remove loose jewelry so that they do not knock over equipment, get caught in moving parts, or come into contact with hazardous materials or electrical connections.
- Do not wear open-toed shoes, sandals, or canvas shoes in the lab.
- When outside for lab, wear long sleeves, long pants, socks, and closed shoes.

Glassware Safety

- Inspect glassware before use; do not use chipped or cracked glassware.
- Use heat-resistant glassware for heating materials or storing hot liquids.
- Notify your teacher immediately if a piece of glassware or a light bulb breaks.

Sharp-Object Safety

- Use extreme care when handling all sharp and pointed instruments.
- Cut objects on a suitable surface, always in a direction away from your body.
- Be aware of sharp objects or edges on equipment or apparatus.

Chemical Safety

- If a chemical gets on your skin, on your clothing, or in your eyes, rinse it immediately (shower, faucet or eyewash fountain) and alert your teacher.
- Do not clean up spilled chemicals yourself unless your teacher directs you to do so.
- Do not inhale any gas or vapor unless your teacher directs you to do so.
- Handle materials that emit vapors or gases in a well-ventilated area.

Name ______________________________ Class ________________ Date ______________

Safety Symbols continued

	**Electrical Safety** • Do not use equipment with frayed electrical cords or loose plugs. • Fasten electrical cords to work surfaces by using tape. • Do not use electrical equipment near water or when clothing or hands are wet. • Hold the plug housing when you plug in or unplug equipment. • Be aware that wire coils in electrical circuits may heat up rapidly.
	**Heating Safety** • Be aware of any source of flames, sparks, or heat (such as open flames, heating coils, or hot plates) before working with any flammable substances. • Avoid using open flames. • Know the location of lab fire extinguishers and fire-safety blankets. • Know your school's fire-evacuation routes. • If your clothing catches on fire, walk to the lab shower to put out the fire. • Never leave a hot plate unattended while it is turned on or while it is cooling. • Use tongs or appropriate insulated holders when handling heated objects. • Allow all equipment to cool before storing it.
	**Plant Safety** • Do not eat any part of a plant or plant seed. • When outside, do not pick any wild plants unless your teacher instructs you to do so. • Wash your hands thoroughly after handling any part of a plant.
	**Animal Safety** • Handle animals only as your teacher directs. • Treat animals carefully and respectfully. • Wash your hands thoroughly after handling any animal.
	**Proper Waste Disposal** • Clean and sanitize all work surfaces and personal protective equipment after each lab period as directed by your teacher. • Dispose of hazardous materials only as directed by your teacher. • Dispose of sharp objects (such as broken glass) in the appropriate sharps or broken glass container as directed by your teacher.
	**Hygienic Care** • Keep your hands away from your face while you are working on any activity. • Wash your hands thoroughly before you leave the lab or after any activity. • Remove contaminated clothing immediately.

Safety in the Laboratory

1. **Always wear a lab apron and safety goggles.** Wear these safety devices whenever you are in the lab, not just when you are working on an experiment.
2. **No contact lenses in the lab.** Contact lenses should not be worn during any investigations in which you are using chemicals (even if you are wearing goggles). In the event of an accident, chemicals can get behind contact lenses and cause serious damage before the lenses can be removed. If your doctor requires that you wear contact lenses instead of glasses, you should wear eye-cup safety goggles in the lab. Ask your doctor or your teacher how to use this very important and special eye protection.
3. **Personal apparel should be appropriate for laboratory work.** On lab days, avoid wearing long necklaces, dangling bracelets, bulky jewelry, and bulky or loose-fitting clothing. Long hair should be tied back. Loose, flopping, or dangling items may get caught in moving parts, accidentally contact electrical connections, or interfere with the investigation in some potentially hazardous manner. In addition, chemical fumes may react with some jewelry, such as pearls, and ruin them. Cotton clothing is preferable to wool, nylon, or polyesters. Wear shoes that will protect your feet from chemical spills and falling objects— no open-toed shoes or sandals and no shoes with woven leather straps.
4. **NEVER work alone in the laboratory.** Work in the lab only while supervised by your teacher. Do not leave equipment unattended while it is in operation.
5. **Only books and notebooks needed for the activity should be in the lab.** Only the lab notebook and perhaps the textbook should be used. Keep other books, backpacks, purses, and similar items in your desk, locker, or designated storage area.
6. **Read the entire activity before entering the lab.** Your teacher will review any applicable safety precautions before you begin the lab activity. If you are not sure of something, ask your teacher about it.
7. Always heed safety symbols and cautions in the instructions for the experiments, in handouts, and on posters in the room, and always heed cautions given verbally by your teacher. They are provided for your safety.
8. Know the proper fire drill procedures and the locations of fire exits and emergency equipment. Make sure you know the procedures to follow in case of a fire or other emergency.
9. **If your clothing catches on fire, do not run;** WALK to the safety shower, stand under the showerhead, and turn the water on. Call to your teacher while you do this.
10. **Report all accidents to the teacher** IMMEDIATELY, no matter how minor. In addition, if you get a headache or feel ill or dizzy, tell your teacher immediately.

11. **Report all spills to your teacher immediately.** Call your teacher, rather than cleaning a spill yourself. Your teacher will tell you if it is safe for you to clean up the spill. If it is not safe for you to clean up the spill, your teacher will know how the spill should be cleaned up safely.
12. If a lab directs you to design your own experiments, procedures must be approved by your teacher BEFORE you begin work.
13. DO NOT perform unauthorized experiments or use equipment or apparatus in a manner for which they were not intended. Use only materials and equipment listed in the activity equipment list or authorized by your teacher. Steps in a procedure should only be performed as described in the lab manual or as approved by your teacher.
14. **Stay alert while in the lab, and proceed with caution.** Be aware of others near you or your equipment when you are proceeding with the experiment. If you are not sure of how to proceed, ask your teacher for help.
15. **Horseplay in the lab is very dangerous.** Laboratory equipment and apparatus are not toys; never play in the lab or use lab time or equipment for anything other than their intended purpose.
16. Food, beverages, and chewing gum are NEVER permitted in the laboratory.
17. **NEVER taste chemicals.** Do not touch chemicals or allow them to contact areas of bare skin.
18. **Use extreme CAUTION when working with hot plates or other heating devices.** Keep your head, hands, hair, and clothing away from the flame or heating area, and turn the devices off when they are not in use. Remember that metal surfaces connected to the heated area will become hot by conduction. Gas burners should be lit only with a spark lighter. Make sure all heating devices and gas valves are turned off before leaving the laboratory. Never leave a hot plate or other heating device unattended when it is in use. Remember that many metal, ceramic, and glass items do not always look hot when they are heated. Allow all items to cool before storing them.
19. **Exercise caution when working with electrical equipment.** Do not use electrical equipment that has frayed or twisted wires. Be sure your hands are dry before you use electrical equipment. Do not let electrical cords dangle from work stations; dangling cords can cause tripping or electrical shocks.
20. **Keep work areas and apparatus clean and neat.** Always clean up any clutter made during the course of lab work, rearrange apparatus in an orderly manner, and report any damaged or missing items.
21. Always thoroughly wash your hands with soap and water at the conclusion of each investigation.

Name ______________________ Class ______________ Date ______________

Safety in the Field

Activities conducted outdoors require some advance planning to ensure a safe environment. The following general guidelines should be followed for fieldwork.

1. Know your mission. Your teacher will tell you the goal of the field trip in advance. Be sure to have your permission slip approved before the trip, and check to be sure that you have all necessary supplies for the day's activity.
2. Find out about on-site hazards before setting out. Determine whether poisonous plants or dangerous animals are likely to be present where you are going. Know how to identify these hazards. Find out about other hazards, such as steep or slippery terrain.
3. Wear protective clothing. Dress in a manner that will keep you warm, comfortable, and dry. Decide in advance whether you will need sunglasses, a hat, gloves, boots, or rain gear to suit the terrain and local weather conditions.
4. Do not approach or touch wild animals. If you see a threatening animal, call your teacher immediately. Avoid any living thing that may sting, bite, scratch, or otherwise cause injury.
5. Do not touch wild plants or pick wildflowers unless specifically instructed to do so by your teacher. Many wild plants can be irritating or toxic. Never taste any wild plant.
6. Do not wander away from others. Travel with a partner at all times. Stay within an area where you can be seen or heard in case you run into trouble.
7. Report all hazards or accidents to your teacher immediately. Even if the incident seems unimportant, let your teacher know what happened.
8. Maintain the safety of the environment. Do not remove anything from the field site without your teacher's permission. Stay on trails, when possible, to avoid trampling delicate vegetation. Never leave garbage behind at a field site. Leave natural areas as you found them.

Laboratory Techniques

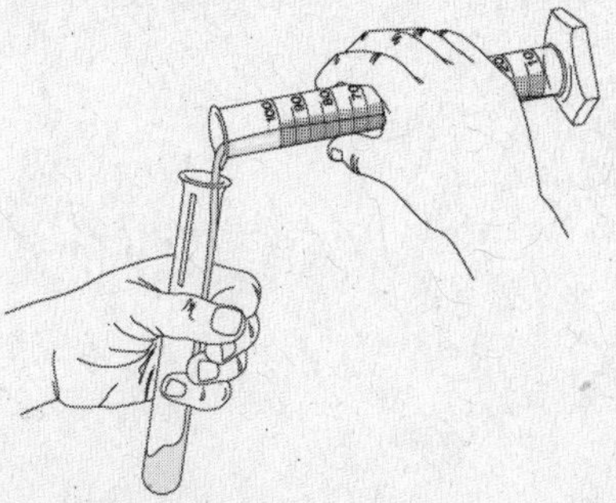

Figure A

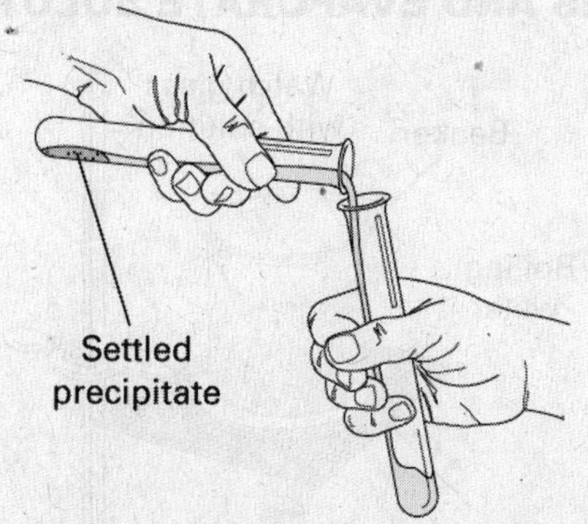

Figure B

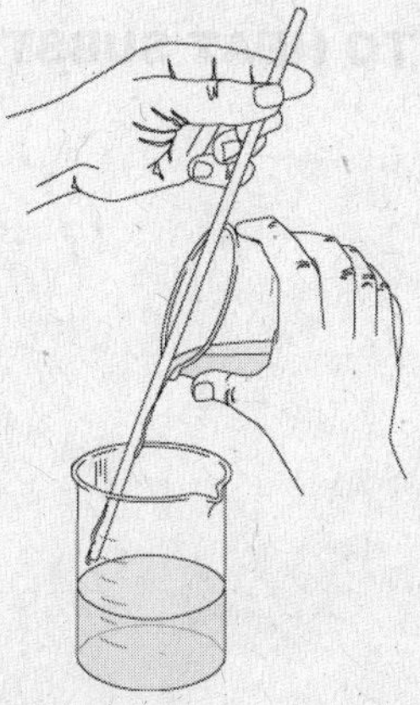

Figure C

HOW TO DECANT AND TRANSFER LIQUIDS

1. The safest way to transfer a liquid from a graduated cylinder to a test tube is shown in **Figure A**. The liquid is transferred at arm's length, with the elbows slightly bent. This position enables you to see what you are doing while maintaining steady control of the equipment.
2. Sometimes, liquids contain particles of insoluble solids that sink to the bottom of a test tube or beaker. Use one of the methods shown above to separate a supernatant (the clear fluid) from insoluble solids.

   a. **Figure B** shows the proper method of decanting a supernatant liquid from a test tube.

   b. **Figure C** shows the proper method of decanting a supernatant liquid from a beaker by using a stirring rod. The rod should touch the wall of the receiving container. Hold the stirring rod against the lip of the beaker containing the supernatant. As you pour, the liquid will run down the rod and fall into the beaker resting below. When you use this method, the liquid will not run down the side of the beaker from which you are pouring.

Laboratory Techniques continued

HOW TO HEAT SUBSTANCES AND EVAPORATE SOLUTIONS

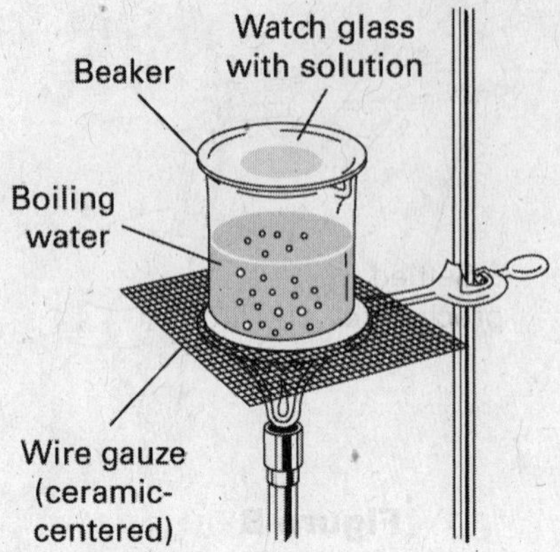

FIGURE D

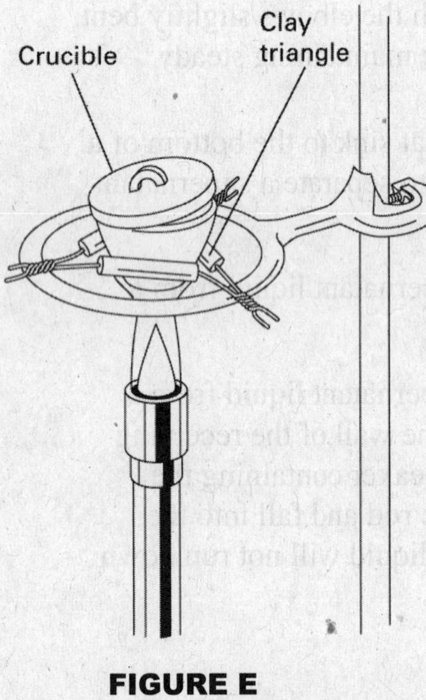

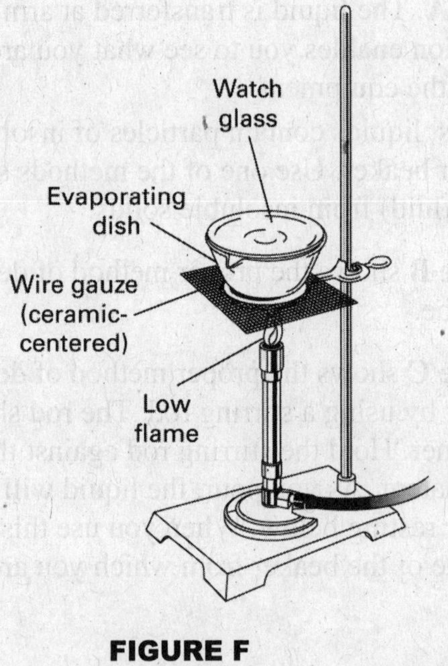

FIGURE E **FIGURE F**

1. Use care in selecting glassware for high-temperature heating. The glassware should be heat resistant.
2. When heating glassware by using a gas flame, use a ceramic-centered wire gauze to protect glassware from direct contact with the flame. Wire gauzes can withstand extremely high temperatures and will help prevent glassware from breaking. **Figure D** shows the proper setup for evaporating a solution over a water bath.
3. In some experiments, you are required to heat a substance to high temperatures in a porcelain crucible. Figure E shows the proper apparatus setup used to accomplish this task.
4. **Figure F** shows the proper setup for evaporating a solution in a porcelain evaporating dish with a watch glass cover that prevents spattering.

5. Glassware, porcelain, and iron rings that have been heated may look cool after they are removed from a heat source, but these items can still burn your skin even after several minutes of cooling. Use tongs, test-tube holders, or heat-resistant mitts and pads whenever you handle these pieces of apparatus.
6. You can test the temperature of beakers, ring stands, wire gauzes, or other pieces of apparatus that have been heated by holding the back of your hand close to their surfaces before grasping them. You will be able to feel any energy as heat generated from the hot surfaces. DO NOT TOUCH THE APPARATUS. Allow plenty of time for the apparatus to cool before handling.

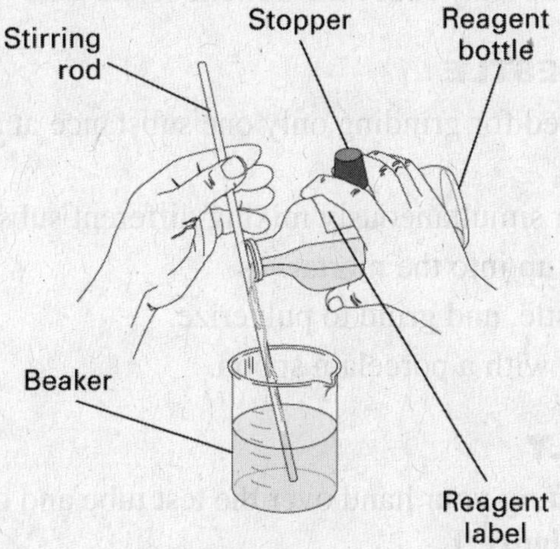

FIGURE G

HOW TO POUR LIQUID FROM A REAGENT BOTTLE

1. Read the label at least three times before using the contents of a reagent bottle.
2. Never lay the stopper of a reagent bottle on the lab table.
3. When pouring a caustic or corrosive liquid into a beaker, use a stirring rod to avoid drips and spills. Hold the stirring rod against the lip of the reagent bottle. Estimate the amount of liquid you need, and pour this amount along the rod, into the beaker. See **Figure G**.
4. Extra precaution should be taken when handling a bottle of acid. Remember the following important rules: Never add water to any concentrated acid, particularly sulfuric acid, because the mixture can splash and will generate a lot of energy as heat. To dilute any acid, add the acid to water in small quantities while stirring slowly. Remember the "triple A's"—*Always Add Acid* to water.
5. Examine the outside of the reagent bottle for any liquid that has dripped down the bottle or spilled on the counter top. Your teacher will show you the proper procedures for cleaning up a chemical spill.
6. Never pour reagents back into stock bottles. At the end of the experiment, your teacher will tell you how to dispose of any excess chemicals.

HOW TO HEAT MATERIAL IN A TEST TUBE

1. Check to see that the test tube is heat resistant.
2. Always use a test tube holder or clamp when heating a test tube.
3. Never point a heated test tube at anyone, because the liquid may splash out of the test tube.
4. Never look down into the test tube while heating it.
5. Heat the test tube from the upper portions of the tube downward, and continuously move the test tube, as shown in **Figure H**. Do not heat any one spot on the test tube. Otherwise, a pressure buildup may cause the bottom of the tube to blow out.

HOW TO USE A MORTAR AND PESTLE

1. A mortar and pestle should be used for grinding only one substance at a time. See **Figure I**.
2. Never use a mortar and pestle for simultaneously mixing different substances.
3. Place the substance to be broken up into the mortar.
4. Pound the substance with the pestle, and grind to pulverize.
5. Remove the powdered substance with a porcelain spoon.

HOW TO DETECT ODORS SAFELY

1. Test for the odor of gases by wafting your hand over the test tube and cautiously sniffing the fumes as shown in **Figure J**.
2. Do not inhale any fumes directly.
3. Use a fume hood whenever poisonous or irritating fumes are present. DO NOT waft and sniff poisonous or irritating fumes.

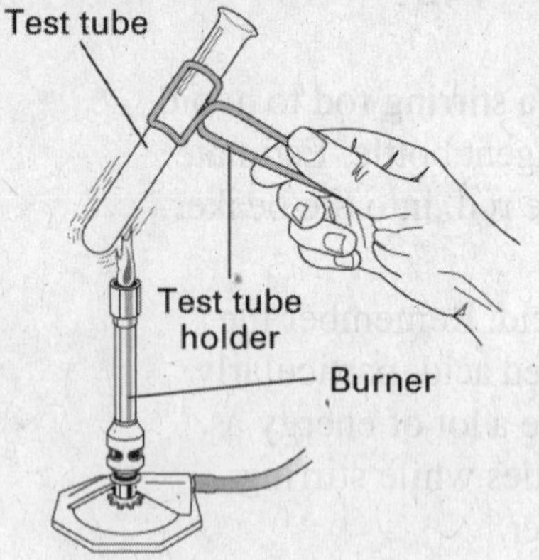

FIGURE H

FIGURE I

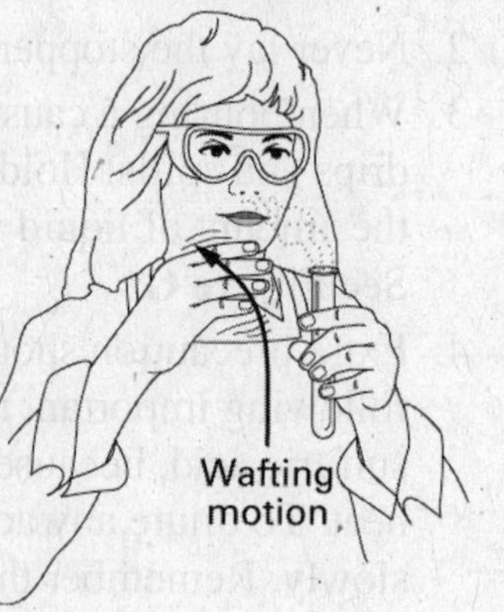

FIGURE J

Name ______________________ Class ______________ Date ______________

Student Safety Quiz

Circle the letter of the BEST answer.

1. Before starting an investigation or lab procedure, you should
   a. try an experiment of your own
   b. open all containers and packages
   c. read all directions and make sure you understand them
   d. handle all the equipment to become familiar with it

2. When pouring chemicals between containers, you should hold the containers over
   a. the floor or a waste basket
   b. a fire blanket or an oven mitt
   c. an eyewash station or a water fountain
   d. a sink or your work area

3. If you get hurt or injured in any way, you should
   a. tell your teacher immediately
   b. find bandages or a first aid kit
   c. go to the principal's office
   d. get help after you finish the lab

4. If your glassware is chipped or broken, you should
   a. use it only for solid materials
   b. give it to your teacher
   c. put it back into the storage cabinet
   d. increase the damage so that it is obvious

5. If you have unused chemicals after finishing a procedure, you should
   a. pour them down a sink or drain
   b. mix them all together in a bucket
   c. put them back into their original containers
   d. throw them away where your teacher tells you to

6. If electrical equipment has a frayed cord, you should
   a. unplug the equipment by pulling on the cord
   b. let the cord hang over the side of a counter or table
   c. tell your teacher about the problem immediately
   d. wrap tape around the cord to repair it
7. If you need to determine the odor of a chemical or a solution, you should
   a. use your hand to bring fumes from the container to your nose
   b. bring the container under your nose and inhale deeply
   c. tell your teacher immediately
   d. use odor-sensing equipment
8. When working with materials that might fly into the air and hurt someone's eye, you should wear
   a. goggles
   b. an apron
   c. gloves
   d. a hat
9. Before doing experiments involving a heat source, you should know the location of the
   a. door
   b. windows
   c. fire extinguisher
   d. overhead lights
10. If you get a chemical in your eye, you should
    a. wash your hands immediately
    b. put the lid back on the chemical container
    c. wait to see if your eye becomes irritated
    d. use the eyewash right away

11. When working with a flame or heat source, you should
    a. tie back long hair or hair that hangs in front of your eyes
    b. heat substances or objects inside a closed container
    c. touch an object with your bare hand to see how hot it is
    d. throw hot objects into the trash when you are done with them

12. As you cut with a knife or other sharp instrument, you should move the instrument
    a. toward you
    b. away from you
    c. vertically
    d. horizontally

Name ______________________________ Class ________________ Date ____________________

LAB SAFETY QUIZ

Answer Key

1. C	5. D	9. C
2. D	6. C	10. D
3. A	7. A	11. A
4. B	8. A	12. B

Student Safety Contract

Read carefully the Student Safety Contract below. Then, fill in your name in the first blank, date the contract, and sign it.

Student Safety Contract

I will

- read the lab investigation before coming to class
- wear personal protective equipment as directed to protect my eyes, face, hands, and body while conducting class activities
- follow all instructions given by the teacher
- conduct myself in a responsible manner at all times in a laboratory situation

I, ____, have read and agree to abide by the safety regulations as set forth above and any additional printed instructions provided by my teacher or the school district.

I agree to follow all other written and oral instructions given in class.

Signature: ________________________________

Date: ________________________________

QUICK LAB DIRECTED Inquiry

Investigate Changing Positions GENERAL

Student pairs
15 minutes

LAB RATINGS LESS ← → MORE

Teacher Prep — 1
Student Setup — 1
Cleanup — 1

MATERIALS
For each pair
- ball, wiffle

For each student
- safety goggles

My Notes

SAFETY INFORMATION

Remind students to review all safety cautions and icons before beginning this lab. Students should use caution when walking and throwing a ball; this activity should be conducted in an open area where students will not run into each other.

TEACHER NOTES

In this activity, students will investigate how a change in reference point changes how an object appears to move. You may wish to have students complete this activity outside or in a large area where there is plenty of space to move. Instruct students to throw the balls to about eye level; wildly high throws will be too hard to catch and will distract students from making detailed observations about the position of the ball.

Tip You may wish to model an appropriate throw to your students so they can see you walking forward and throwing the ball to yourself.

Skills Focus Making Observations, Creating Sketches, Applying Concepts

MODIFICATION FOR GUIDED Inquiry

Instruct students to complete the first part of the lab, viewing a ball that they throw while walking, as instructed in the student datasheet. Then, challenge student pairs to brainstorm how they could change the reference point in order to change the relative position of the ball. Pairs should gain teacher approval for their ideas and then carry out a second investigation to see how the position of the ball changes from a different reference point.

Quick Lab continued

Answer Key

3. Accept all reasonable answers. Students should see that their own ball appeared to move more or less straight up and down, while their partner's ball appeared to move in a series of arcs. These findings should be displayed in their sketches.
4. Accept all reasonable answers and sketches. Students should explain what they observed and what they sketched in the table.
5. Sample answer: When I was walking and tossing the ball, I couldn't see the effect of my forward motion because the ball stayed the same distance away from me. My reference point was constantly changing, and the ball only appeared to move vertically. When my partner tossed the ball, my reference point stayed the same as my partner moved, so I could see the forward motion of the ball. I could see both vertical and horizontal movement of the ball.
6. Accept all reasonable answers. The person would see the ball go up and down. As the student tossing the ball drew nearer, the ball would also appear to increase in size, but the person standing in front wouldn't see any other horizontal movement of the ball.

Name ______________________________ Class ________________ Date ______________________

QUICK LAB DIRECTED *Inquiry*

Investigate Changing Positions

In this lab, you will investigate how a change in your reference point affects how a ball appears to move. First, you will toss the ball to yourself while you are walking. Then, you'll stay in one place and watch your partner toss the ball while they are walking.

OBJECTIVE

- Observe how the position of an object seems to change as the reference point changes.

MATERIALS

For each pair
- ball, wiffle

For each student
- safety goggles

PROCEDURE

1. Begin walking while tossing a ball straight up and catching it as it falls back toward your hand. Continue walking and tossing the ball while observing the changes in position of the ball for a distance of about 4 meters (m).

2. Make a sketch from your reference point showing how the position of the ball changed. Draw your sketch in the table below.

3. Have your partner complete Step 1 while you remain stationary. Your partner should walk past you throwing the ball. Observe how the position of the ball changes from your reference point. In the table below, draw a sketch from your new reference point showing how the position of the ball changed.

Ball's movement: Throwing to myself	Ball's movement: Viewing partner

4. Compare your two sketches. How was the change in position of the ball you tossed different from the change in position that your partner tossed? Explain.

____

____

Quick Lab continued

5. The ball moved in approximately the same way both times. How did your reference point affect what you observed?

____

____

____

____

6. Imagine repeating the investigation a third time. This time, a person is standing approximately 5 m directly in front of you, and you are walking toward that person tossing the ball. How would the ball appear to the person standing before you?

____

____

____

QUICK LAB GUIDED *Inquiry*

Create a Distance-Time Graph GENERAL

Individual student
25 minutes

LAB RATINGS

LESS ◄──► MORE

Teacher Prep — 3
Student Setup — 1
Cleanup — 1

MATERIALS

For each student

- index card (with pre-prepared distance-time scenario)
- paper, graphing
- pencils, colored (2)

My Notes

TEACHER NOTES

In this activity, students will create a distance-time graph. They should already be familiar with the concept, but you may want to show them an example of a distance-time graph and describe how to read it. Prior to the lesson, copy the four scenarios listed below onto index cards; each student should receive one index card (you may also create original scenarios for your students if you wish to have more than four scenarios). Students will create their distance-time graph and then partner with a student who has a different scenario. They will study each other's distance-time graphs and determine when the object had the greatest and least speed (steepest slope versus less steep or no slope).

Sample Scenario #1: A runner is racing in a 10-kilometer (km) race. The runner travels the first 2 km in 12 minutes (min). Then the runner stops for 2 min to have a drink of water. He begins running again, and covers the next kilometer in 5 min. The following 3 km have the same pace: 6 minutes per kilometer (min/km). The runner again pauses to tie his shoe; he is paused for 1.5 min. He has 4 remaining km to go. When he starts running again, he runs 1 km in 5 min, but the remaining 3 km are each 1 min slower than the one before (6 min, 7 min, and 8 min, respectively). Create a distance-time graph to show the runner's speed.

Sample Scenario #2: A bus driver is driving his bus on its typical morning route, which is 12 km long. The bus driver leaves the station and travels 2 km to his first stop; it takes him 3 min to get there, and he has to stop halfway to his first stop to pause for 30 seconds at a stoplight. He pauses at his first stop for 1 min to let people on the bus. He then drives 3 km in 3 min, with no stops. He stops at the second bus stop for 1.5 min to let people on and off, then drives 2 km in 2 min, before stopping at a red light for 30 seconds. The bus driver then drives 1 km in 2 min, and stops at the third stop. It takes 2 min for people to get on and off the bus. The driver then takes the interstate straight to the fourth stop, 4 km away. He travels the 4 km in 2 min, with no pauses. Finally, he stops at the fourth bus stop and everybody gets off the bus. Create a distance-time graph to show the speed of the bus.

Quick Lab continued

Sample Scenario #3: A child is riding her bike to school. It's a 4 km journey, and it takes her a total of 18 min. She leaves the house and rides 1 km in 3 min, with no stops. She then pauses at a red light for 1 min. When it turns green, she resumes riding her bike. The road slopes downhill for a bit, and she covers 1 km in 2 min. She stops at the bottom of the hill for 4 min to visit with a friend who is walking to school. For a while, she rides her bike at the same speed as her walking friend. Together, they cover 1 km in 7 min. The last kilometer is also downhill, so she rides ahead of her friend and zips down the hill to school. She covers the last kilometer in 1 min, and arrives at the school. Create a distance-time graph to show her speed.

Sample Scenario #4: A mother goes on a walk with her young child. They leave the house and walk 25 meters (m) in 2 min until the child is distracted by a flower and they stop for 1 min. They resume walking for 3 min and cover another 25 m in this time. Then, they start running. They run 50 m in 1 min. They stop at the neighborhood playground for 10 min before they start walking back home. They walk 50 m in 4 min, then stop for 3 min because the child falls down. They then walk quickly back home, covering 50 m in 2 min, stopping only once they have reached their house. Create a distance-time graph to show the speed of the mother and child.

Tip If your students are unfamiliar with the concept of distance-time graphs, model the process by walking through one of the sample scenarios, drawing a distance-time graph on graph paper as you read the example. If you think some students might struggle with this activity, Scenario #4 is less complex than the other three, and may be suitable for these students.

Skills Focus Creating Graphs, Following Written Directions, Working Independently

MODIFICATION FOR INDEPENDENT Inquiry

Instruct students to work with a partner. Each partner will brainstorm a different scenario to show distance traveled over time. Partners will then swap scenarios and create a distance-time graph of their partner's scenario. They can then swap completed graphs and locate the places in their partner's graph with the greatest and least speed (as described in the student datasheet below).

Answer Key

5. Accept all reasonable answers. Students should identify the place in the graph with the steepest slope, as this indicates more distance traveled in less time. Students should also record the speed for this section, such as 3 km/min.
6. Accept all reasonable answers. Students should identify a place in the graph with a slope of zero (a flat line). All of the provided scenarios include sections where the object in the graph is not moving.
7. Sample answer: A steep line on the graph indicates that the object is moving faster. **Teacher Prompt** Does the direction that the object is moving matter? Can we tell what direction the object is moving by looking at a distance-time graph?
8. Sample answer: A flat line on the graph indicates that the object is not moving. Time is still passing, but the object isn't covering any distance.

QUICK LAB GUIDED Inquiry

Create a Distance-Time Graph

In this lab, you will create a distance-time graph to show the speed of an object, or its distance traveled over time. Your teacher will give you an index card with a written scenario; you'll turn that scenario into a distance-time graph. When you finish, you'll swap your graph with a classmate, and analyze the graph they created.

OBJECTIVES

- Create a distance-time graph.
- Understand that the slope of the line on a distance-time graph directly relates to speed.

MATERIALS

For each student

- index card (with pre-prepared distance-time scenario)
- paper, graphing
- pencils, colored (2)

PROCEDURE

1. Your teacher will give you an index card with a scenario on it. Read the card carefully.
2. Use the graph paper to create a distance-time graph to show how the object(s) in your scenario move(s) over time. Remember that the *y*-axis represents the distance traveled by an object, and the *x*-axis represents time. Include the appropriate units on your graph.
3. When you have finished your graph, find a partner who graphed a different scenario. Swap distance-time graphs with your partner.
4. Study your partner's distance-time graph. Use a pencil of one color to circle the point on the graph where the object had the greatest speed. Use a pencil of a different color to circle a point on the graph where the object had the least speed.
5. Answer the following questions while looking at your partner's distance-time graph. At what point in the graph did the object have the most speed? What was the speed?

____

____

Quick Lab continued

6. At what point in the graph did the object have the least speed? What was the speed?

____

____

7. What does a steep slope on a distance-time graph indicate?

____

8. How would you describe the motion of an object when there is a flat line on the distance-time graph?

____

S.T.E.M. LAB GUIDED Inquiry **AND** INDEPENDENT Inquiry

Investigate Average Speed GENERAL

Individual student
45 minutes

LAB RATINGS

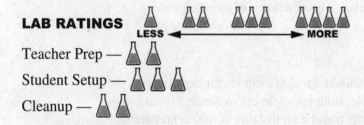

LESS ⟷ MORE

Teacher Prep — 2
Student Setup — 3
Cleanup — 2

SAFETY INFORMATION

Remind students to review all safety cautions and icons before beginning this lab. Students should wear safety gloves when working with modeling clay. if they use scissors to make holes in the film container lids; hard plastic can be difficult to work with.

MATERIALS

For each student

- balance
- board, wood
- books (4–5)
- clay, modeling
- film canister lids (4)
- ruler
- safety goggles
- scissors
- stopwatch
- straw
- string
- toothpicks (2-4)

TEACHER NOTES

In this activity, students will build simple model cars, which they will then race against a classmate's car. They will design their own procedures for testing the speed of the cars, but in general, most students will create a ramp where the cars will start and measure a distance for the cars to travel. They'll then use the stopwatch to time how long it takes each car to travel the distance. Students can have their cars race on any flat, smooth surface, such as the floor or the top of a table. You may use other materials that you have available for students to use to construct their model cars.

Tip You may want to introduce a common measure of speed, such as kilometers per hour to help students see that average speed is a widely used measurement that helps explain how objects travel.

Student Tip This activity will help you understand that an object's average speed may be faster or slower at certain points.

Skills Focus Building Models, Controlling Variables, Analyzing Results

My Notes

MODIFICATION FOR DIRECTED Inquiry

Rather than challenging students to design their own cars, instruct all students to build the same model car. You may want to make a model prior to teaching the lesson and have this on display for students to analyze and copy. Then, have students race their cars against another student's car, and challenge them to explain how one car could go faster than another (there could be slight differences in the construction of the model even though they built the same design). Then, allow students to brainstorm methods to improve the design of their cars to increase the average speed. If time allows, permit students to make modifications to their models and re-race their model cars.

S.T.E.M. Lab continued

Answer Key for GUIDED Inquiry

ASK A QUESTION

1. Accept all reasonable answers. Students should give examples of ways an understanding of speed is used in their lives, such as understanding speed limits for cars, and how knowing the distance traveled over an amount of time helps us understand how fast an object is moving.

DEVELOP A PLAN

4. Accept all reasonable answers. Students should develop methods for investigating the average speed of their model. For example, students might opt to create a ramp using the books and the board and have their cars travel a set distance of 100 centimeters, starting at the top of the ramp. Students should identify how they will control variables, such as the distance and the paths the cars will travel.
Teacher Prompt How will you start your race? Will you push your cars? If so, how will you make sure that the cars are pushed with the same force? Is there another way to start the race without pushing the cars?

MAKE OBSERVATIONS

5. Sample answer:

		Trial 1	Trial 2	Trial 3	Trial 4	Trial 5
Car #1	Time (sec)	3.2	4.1	4	5	4.5
	Distance (cm)	120	120	120	120	120
Car #2	Time (sec)	5.5	5.8	5.1	4.8	5
	Distance (cm)	120	120	120	120	120

ANALYZE THE RESULTS

6. Accept all reasonable answers. Students should write out the average speed for each trial and state which car went faster. For example, in the table above, for Trial 1, Car 1 traveled at an average speed of 120 cm/3.2 sec (or 37.5 cm/sec), and Car 2 traveled at an average speed of 120 cm/5.5 sec (or 21.8 cm/sec). Car 1 traveled faster.

7. Accept all reasonable answers. Students should add up the total number of seconds and the total centimeters and divide it by the total number of trials. In the above example, Car 1 traveled at an overall average speed of 120 cm/4.16 sec (or 37.5 cm/sec), and Car 2 traveled at an overall average speed of 120 cm/ 5.24 sec (or 22.9 cm/sec).

DRAW CONCLUSIONS

8. Sample answer: My car traveled faster when it was on the ramp, moving downward. It moved slower at the end of the race when it was farthest away from the ramp.

S.T.E.M. Lab continued

9. Accept all reasonable answers. Students should critically assess their models and propose changes to the model that might make it faster. Some possible revisions could include making the wheels turn more easily, lowering the center of gravity of the car, or altering the mass of the car.
Teacher Prompt In your revisions, feel free to incorporate material that you didn't originally use in this investigation.

11. Accept all reasonable answers.

Connect TO THE ESSENTIAL QUESTION

12. Sample answer: I need to know both the distance my car traveled and the time it took for the car to travel in order to calculate the average speed of the car. If one of these measurements was missing, I wouldn't be able to figure out the average speed.

Answer Key for INDEPENDENT Inquiry

ASK A QUESTION

1. Accept all reasonable answers. Students should give examples of ways an understanding of speed is used in their lives, such as understanding speed limits for cars, and how knowing the distance traveled over an amount of time helps us understand how fast an object is moving.

DEVELOP A PLAN

4. Accept all reasonable answers. Students should develop methods for investigating the average speed of their model. For example, students might opt to create a ramp using the books and the board, and have their cars travel a set distance of 100 centimeters, starting at the top of the ramp. Students should identify how they will control variables, such as the distance, and the path the cars will travel.
Teacher Prompt How will you start your race? Will you push your cars? If so, how will you make sure that the cars are pushed with the same force? Is there another way to start the race without pushing the cars?

MAKE OBSERVATIONS

5. Sample answer:

		Trial 1	Trial 2	Trial 3	Trial 4	Trial 5
Car #1	Time	3.2	4.1	4	5	4.5
	Distance	120	120	120	120	120
Car #2	Time	5.5	5.8	5.1	4.8	5
	Distance	120	120	120	120	120

S.T.E.M. Lab continued

ANALYZE THE RESULTS

6. Accept all reasonable answers. Students should write out the average speed for each trial, and state which car went faster. For example, in the table above, for Trial 1, Car 1 traveled at an average speed of 120 cm/3.2 sec (or 37.5 cm/sec), and Car 2 traveled at an average speed of 120 cm/5.5 sec (or 21.8 cm/sec). Car 1 traveled faster.

7. Accept all reasonable answers. Students should add up the total number of seconds and the total centimeters, and divide it by the total number of trials. In the above example, Car 1 traveled at an overall average speed of 120 cm/4.16 sec (or 37.5 cm/sec), and Car 2 traveled at an overall average speed of 120 cm/ 5.24 sec (or 22.9 cm/sec).

DRAW CONCLUSIONS

8. Sample answer: My car traveled faster when it was on the ramp, moving downward. It moved slower at the end of the race when it was farthest away from the ramp.

9. Accept all reasonable answers. Students should critically assess their models and propose changes to the model that might make it faster. Some possible revisions could include making the wheels turn more easily, lowering the center of gravity of the car, or altering the mass of the car.
Teacher Prompt In your revisions, feel free to incorporate material that you didn't originally use in this investigation.

11. Accept all reasonable answers.

Connect TO THE ESSENTIAL QUESTION

12. Sample answer: I need to know both the distance my car traveled and the time it took for the car to travel in order to calculate the average speed of the car. If one of these measurements was missing, I wouldn't be able to figure out the average speed.

Name ______________________ Class ______________ Date ______________

S.T.E.M. LAB GUIDED *Inquiry*

Investigate Average Speed

In this lab, you will build a simple model car. You will then race your car against a classmate's car and record the time it took for each car to travel a certain distance. These measurements will help you compute the average speed of your car (and your classmate's). As you design your procedures, keep in mind that the car design should be the only variable you test; this means that all other variables, including slope and distance, should be the same for each trial.

OBJECTIVES

- Design and build a model car to illustrate the concept of speed and average speed.
- Use data collected from an investigation to calculate the average speed of a moving object.

MATERIALS

For each student

- balance
- board, wood
- books (4–5)
- clay, modeling
- film canister lids (4)
- ruler
- safety goggles
- scissors
- stopwatch
- straw
- string
- toothpicks (2-4)

PROCEDURE

ASK A QUESTION

1. Speed is a measure of how fast something moves in a given amount of time. Write down ways that the measurement of speed is used in your life and why it can be important to understand how to compute average speed.

BUILD A MODEL

2. Use the clay, film canister lids, and toothpicks to design a simple model car that rolls when it is pushed. The car should have a total mass of 150 grams (g) or less.

DEVELOP A PLAN

3. Using any or all of the remaining materials, design an experiment to measure and compare the speed of your car with the speed of a classmate's car. The design of the car should be the only variable being tested.

4. Write up your procedure for testing the speed of the two cars. What variables will you control, and how will you make sure your results are valid?

S.T.E.M. Lab continued

MAKE OBSERVATIONS

5 Perform your experiment using your car and another student's car. Record the data you need to calculate the average speed of both cars in the data table below. Remember that average speed is computed using the formula S = d/t.

		Trial 1	Trial 2	Trial 3	Trial 4	Trial 5
Car #1	Time (sec)					
	Distance (cm)					
Car #2	Time (sec)					
	Distance (cm)					

ANALYZE THE RESULTS

6 **Examining Tables** Calculate the average speed for each trial, and record which car went faster. Record your results below.

____

____

____

____

7 **Analyzing Results** Now, record the average speed from all of the trials for both cars. To do this, add up all of the average speeds from each trial (total number of seconds and total number of centimeters) and divide by the number of trials. Show your work. Record the overall average speed for each car below.

____

____

____

____

____

____

____

____

S.T.E.M. Lab continued

DRAW CONCLUSIONS

8 **Explaining Observations** Average speed helps us calculate the speed of an object that may not always be moving at a constant speed. When did you observe your model moving at faster or slower speeds during your experiment?

9 **Analyzing Methods** In this investigation, the only variable affecting the speed of your car was the design of your car. How could you alter the design of your car to increase its average speed?

10 **Evaluating Events** Your teacher may permit you to run the investigation again with your modified model. If so, be sure to record your results and again compute the average speed of each trial for each car and the overall average speed of all of the trials.

11 **Describing Constraints** Imagine your car weighed twice its current weight. How might your results change?

Connect TO THE ESSENTIAL QUESTION

12 **Analyzing Concepts** Analyze how the time, distance, and average speed of your model car are related.

Name ______________________________ Class ________________ Date ________________________

S.T.E.M. LAB INDEPENDENT *Inquiry*

Investigate Average Speed

In this lab, you will use some of the materials to build a model car. You'll then develop methods to investigate the speed of your car, and compare its speed to that of a classmate's model. You'll design the procedures, and you'll develop the methods to display your data.

OBJECTIVES

- Design and build a model car to illustrate the concept of speed and average speed.
- Use data collected from an investigation to calculate the average speed of a moving object.

MATERIALS

For each student

- balance
- board, wood
- books (4–5)
- clay, modeling
- film canister lids (4)
- ruler
- safety goggles
- scissors
- stopwatch
- straw
- string
- toothpicks (2-4)

PROCEDURE

ASK A QUESTION

1 Speed is a measure of how fast something moves in a given amount of time. Write down ways that the measurement of speed is used in your life and why it can be important to understand how to compute average speed.

____

____

____

____

BUILD A MODEL

2 Select at least three different materials from the list to use in constructing a simple model car. The car should have a total mass of 150 grams (g) or less, and should move when pushed.

DEVELOP A PLAN

3 Using any or all of the remaining materials, design an experiment to measure and compare the speed of your car with the speed of a classmate's car. The design of the car should be the only variable being tested.

S.T.E.M. Lab continued

4 Write up your procedure for testing the speed of the two cars. What variables will you control, and how will you make sure your results are valid?

____

____

____

____

____

MAKE OBSERVATIONS

5 Perform your experiment using your car and another student's car. Remember that average speed is computed using the formula S=d/t. Create a table and record the data you need to calculate the average speed of both cars in the space below.

ANALYZE THE RESULTS

6 **Examining Tables** Calculate the average speed for each trial and record which car went faster. Record your results below.

____

____

____

____

S.T.E.M. Lab continued

7 **Analyzing Results** Now, record the average speed from all of the trials for both cars. To do this, add up all of the average speeds from each trial (total time, and total distance) and divide by the number of trials. Show your work. Record the overall average speed for each car below.

____

____

____

DRAW CONCLUSIONS

8 **Explaining Observations** Average speed helps us calculate the speed of an object that may not always be moving at a constant speed. When did your model move at the fastest and slowest speeds?

____

____

9 **Analyzing Methods** In this investigation, the only variable affecting the speed of your car was the design of your car. How could you alter the design of your car to increase its average speed?

____

____

____

10 **Evaluating Events** If you run the investigation again with your modified model, be sure to record and compute the average speed of each trial for each car, and the overall average speed of the trials.

11 **Describing Constraints** Imagine your car weighed twice its current weight. How might your results change?

____

____

Connect TO THE ESSENTIAL QUESTION

12 **Analyzing Concepts** Analyze how the time, distance, and average speed of your model car are related.

____

____

____

QUICK LAB DIRECTED *Inquiry*

Acceleration and Slope BASIC

Small groups

20 minutes

LAB RATINGS

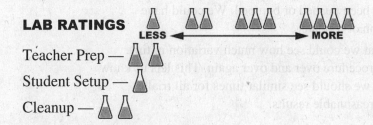

LESS ⟷ MORE

Teacher Prep —

Student Setup —

Cleanup —

MATERIALS

For each group

- books (2)
- calculator
- marble
- metersticks (2)
- ruler, metric
- stopwatch
- tape, masking

For each student

- safety goggles

My Notes

SAFETY INFORMATION

Remind students to review all safety cautions and icons before beginning this lab. Caution students to pick up any marbles that roll onto the floor to avoid someone slipping on them.

TEACHER NOTES

In this activity, students will construct a simple ramp and collect data from a marble rolling down the ramp. They will be able to calculate the marble's average acceleration by assuming an initial velocity of the marble of zero. They will calculate the final velocity of the marble at the end of the ramp by using a stopwatch to determine the time it takes the marble to roll a specified distance along the table after it leaves the ramp. Because they will time the marble's descent down the ramp, students will be able to calculate average acceleration by finding the difference between initial and final velocity of the marble on the ramp and dividing by the time of the marble's descent on the ramp. Students will then vary the slope of their ramp and determine how slope affects average acceleration of the marble.

Students will find that the marble accelerates to a larger extent as the slope of the ramp is increased.

Tip Ask students to think practically about what acceleration means in their everyday lives and what they have experienced when in an analogous situation to the marble. For example, have them compare their experiences on different playground slides of varying height. It might be helpful for students to run through this thought experiment before beginning the activity.

Student Tip What provides energy to make the marble move? How does that change with the slope of the ramp you construct?

Skills Focus Making Predictions, Practicing Lab Techniques

MODIFICATION FOR INDEPENDENT *Inquiry*

Begin by having the students define the terms acceleration and velocity, then have them write down and test their predictions using the marble and ramp setup described above.

Quick Lab continued

Answer Key

9. Sample answer: Acceleration of the marble was greater on the steeper ramp. The final velocity at the end of the ramp is what we measured. Therefore, we could see that acceleration was greater on the steeper ramp because this caused the marble to have a higher velocity once it reached the table.

10. Sample answer: The marble could have been pushed or bumped. We could have stopped or started the stopwatch too soon or too late.

11. Sample answer: We ran five trials so that we could see how much variation in time there was when we repeated the same procedure over and over again. This lets us know if any of our trials was way off because we should see similar times for all trials. It helped us know that we were getting reasonable results.

Name ______________________ Class ______________ Date ______________

QUICK LAB DIRECTED *Inquiry*

Acceleration and Slope

In this lab, you will allow a marble to roll down a ramp and then determine its average acceleration using its initial velocity, final velocity, and the time taken for the marble to roll down the ramp. You will then expand on this investigation by adjusting the slope of the ramp and determining how the average acceleration of the marble changes as a result of the slope change.

OBJECTIVES

- Investigate the effect of ramp slope on an object's average acceleration.
- Evaluate experimental methods.

MATERIALS

For each group
- books (2)
- calculator
- marble
- metersticks (2)
- ruler, metric
- stopwatch
- tape, masking

For each student
- safety goggles

PROCEDURE

1. Tape two metersticks together side by side, leaving a small gap in between for the marble to roll down.
2. Use a book to raise one end of the metersticks off the table slightly.
3. Mark the location where the bottom end of the metersticks touch the table with a piece of masking tape; use the ruler to measure 30 centimeters (cm) from that point and place another piece of tape.

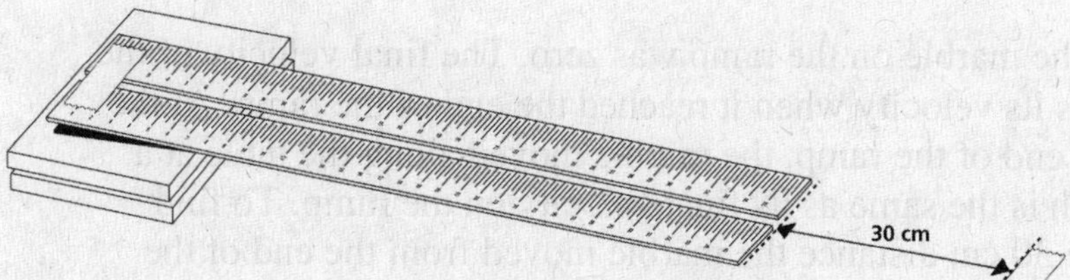

4. How do you predict the marble will behave on the ramp? How do you predict it will behave once it leaves the ramp and begins rolling on the table?

____

____

Quick Lab continued

5. Set the marble at the top of the ramp and release it. Begin timing the marble when you release it. Stop the timer when the marble reaches the end of the ramp. Record the time in the table below. Repeat this step four times for a total of five trials. Record your results in the table and then calculate an average for the five trials.

Trial number	Time on ramp	Time from ramp to tape
1		
2		
3		
4		
5		
Totals		
	Average:	Average:

6. Set the marble at the top of the ramp and release it like before. This time, begin timing when the marble reaches the end of the ramp. Stop timing when the marble reaches the second piece of tape on the table. Record the time in the second column of the table above. Repeat this step four times for a total of five trials. Record your results in the table and then calculate an average for the five trials.

7. The initial velocity of the marble on the ramp was zero. The final velocity of the marble on the ramp was its velocity when it reached the end of the ramp. At the time that it reached the end of the ramp, the marble moved along the table at a constant velocity, which is the same as its final velocity on the ramp. To find this velocity, divide the 30 cm distance the marble moved from the end of the ramp to the tape by the average time it took to roll this distance (the average time in the second column of the data table above.) Show your work in the space below.

8 Now, calculate the average acceleration of the marble on the ramp using the equation, average acceleration = (V_{final} - $V_{initial}$) / time. The time in the denominator is the average time of descent of the marble on the ramp. Show your work in the space below.

9 Raise the height of the ramp and repeat Steps 5–8. Record your results for this new ramp in the data table below. Calculate the average acceleration of the marble on this ramp.

Trial number	Time on ramp	Time from ramp to tape
1		
2		
3		
4		
5		
Totals		
	Average:	Average:

10 How did the average acceleration of the marble differ on the two ramps? Explain.

____

____

11 What errors may have affected your results?

____

____

12 Why did you run multiple trials for each ramp?

____

____

____

QUICK LAB GUIDED *Inquiry*

Mass and Acceleration BASIC

Small groups
25 minutes

LAB RATINGS LESS ⟷ MORE

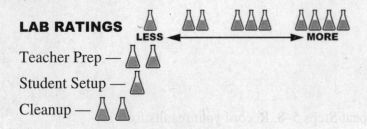

Teacher Prep — 2
Student Setup — 1
Cleanup — 2

MATERIALS

For each group
- mass set
- pulley
- ring stand with clamp
- scissors
- string

For each student
- safety goggles

SAFETY INFORMATION

Remind students to review all safety cautions and icons before beginning this lab. Tell students to make sure that the pulley attached to the ring stand will not topple when they attach the masses.

TEACHER NOTES

In this activity, students will use an Atwood machine to demonstrate the effects of balanced and unbalanced forces on an object. An Atwood machine is a single pulley with a single string looped over it. Two masses are attached to opposite ends of the string, allowing the masses to hang freely. With equal masses, there will be no motion. With one mass increased, students will notice acceleration in the direction of the larger mass. Students will then move on to explore this further by observing that decreasing the smaller mass leads to an increase in its acceleration in the direction of the larger mass. Note that this activity does not allow students a way to calculate acceleration, but can provide a way for students to qualitatively explore the concept of acceleration.

Tip Be sure that students understand the concept of acceleration (the rate of change of the velocity) before they carry out this activity.

Student Tip Compare the movement of the system when the masses are equal to the movement when the masses differ. What do you notice? How might this movement change the more the masses differ from each other?

Skills Focus Making Predictions, Practicing Lab Techniques

My Notes

MODIFICATION FOR INDEPENDENT *Inquiry*

Have students develop their own questions related to acceleration and motion. Students should design controlled experiments to answer their questions. Allow students to carry out all reasonable procedures. They should share their results with the class.

Quick Lab continued

Answer Key

2. Sample answer: No change occurs. The two masses remain in their balanced position.
3. Sample answer: The difference in mass causes the smaller mass to accelerate in the direction of the larger mass.
4. Accept all reasonable plans. Sample answer: We will gradually decrease the mass on one side of the pulley to observe how the acceleration of the system changes.
5. Accept all reasonable answers. Students should observe an increase in acceleration as the smaller mass is made smaller and smaller.
6. Sample answer: If we hold one mass constant and decrease the mass on the other side, the smaller mass accelerates in the direction of the larger mass. As the smaller mass is made smaller and smaller, it accelerates to a greater extent as its mass gets smaller.

Name ______________________________ Class ________________ Date ______________________

QUICK LAB GUIDED *Inquiry*

Mass and Acceleration

In this activity, you will begin by investigating the effects of balanced forces acting on an object. Then you will change the setup so that the forces are no longer balanced. You will explore acceleration as you continue to change this setup.

OBJECTIVES

- Explore the effect of mass on the acceleration of an object.

MATERIALS

For each group

- mass set
- pulley
- ring stand with clamp
- scissors
- string

For each student

- safety goggles

PROCEDURE

1. Connect the pulley to the ring stand. Run a piece of string over the wheel in the pulley so that the two ends of the string hang down from the sides of the pulley. There should be about the same amount of string on each side of the pulley. Tie a loop in each end of the string to hang the masses from.

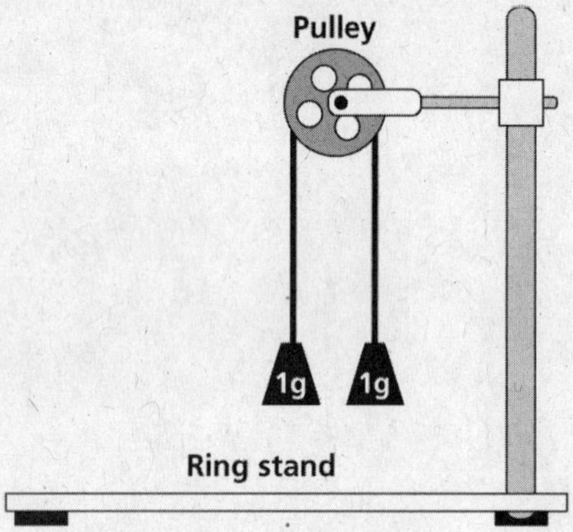

2. Place the two largest masses of equal size on the ends of the string, and orient them on either side of the pulley so that they are hanging at the same vertical position. Then let go of them at the same time. What do you observe?

____

____

3. Replace one of the masses with the next smaller size mass. Orient the two masses on either side of the pulley so that they are hanging at the same vertical position. Then let go of them at the same time. What do you observe?

____

____

Quick Lab continued

4 Based on what you observed in Step 3, develop a plan to continue decreasing the mass on one side of the system and to observe how that affects the acceleration of the smaller mass in the direction of the larger mass. Summarize your plan in a sentence below.

____

____

5 Ask your teacher to approve your plan and then carry it out. Record your observations in the space below.

6 What do you conclude about the effects of decreasing mass on acceleration of an object?

____

____

____

S.T.E.M. LAB GUIDED *Inquiry* **AND** INDEPENDENT *Inquiry*

Investigate Acceleration GENERAL

Small groups

45 minutes

LAB RATINGS LESS ⟷ MORE

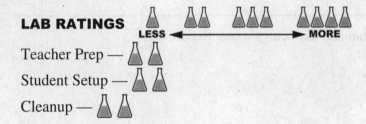

Teacher Prep — 2

Student Setup — 2

Cleanup — 2

MATERIALS

For each group
- cardboard
- glue
- scissors
- string
- washer

For each student
- safety goggles

My Notes

SAFETY INFORMATION

Remind students to review all safety cautions and icons before beginning this lab. Remind students to use care when handling scissors, especially when poking a hole through the accelerometer.

TEACHER NOTES

In this activity, students will investigate acceleration by constructing a simple accelerometer and observing how it behaves as they move backward or forward.

You may wish to make photocopies of the accelerometer template to distribute to each group. These can be glued onto cardboard that is stiff but not too thick so as to allow students to cut around the outside edges of the template. Students then poke a hole through the circle indicated on the template and thread a string through the hole. They then tie a metal washer or other weight to the string so that the weight will hang vertically when the accelerometer is at rest.

Tip Have students develop their own definitions of acceleration and validate those definitions against what they learn during the lab.

Student Tip As you work through the lab, consider what you learn and how it might link into other subjects. How many topics can you think of where acceleration makes a difference?

Skills Focus Constructing Tools, Making Predictions, Making Observations

MODIFICATION FOR DIRECTED *Inquiry*

Work as a class to explore the use of the accelerometer to analyze the various movements described in the procedure. As the class works as a whole, provide immediate feedback and support to students who may not be accurately observing the changes indicated by the accelerometer.

S.T.E.M. Lab continued

Answer Key for GUIDED Inquiry

MAKE OBSERVATIONS

2. Sample answer: The string and weight do not move and hang vertically at the 0 m/s^2 mark on the accelerometer.

3. Sample answer: We observe positive acceleration when we move the tool faster and negative acceleration when we slow its movement.

4. Sample answer: When we move the tool backward, the weight and string move in the opposite direction as when we move it forward.

FORM A PREDICTION

5. Sample answer: We predict that the accelerometer will show a positive acceleration when we move forward faster and faster. If we walk steadily, we predict that the accelerometer will show no acceleration. If we slow down, we think the accelerometer will show a negative acceleration.

MAKE OBSERVATIONS

6. See sample answer in the table below.

7. See sample answer in the table below.

8. See sample answer in the table below.

MOVEMENT OF STRING

While speeding up	While walking steadily	While slowing down
Rearward/positive	No change	Forward/negative

ANALYZE THE RESULTS

9. Sample answer: We experienced acceleration any time we changed speeds.

10. Answers will vary. Students should observe the largest acceleration when they have the greatest change in speed.

11. Sample answer: Acceleration is a change in speed or a change in direction over time.

Connect TO THE ESSENTIAL QUESTION

12. Answers will vary but should demonstrate comprehension of the accelerometer's purpose as well as its limitations, For example, students could spin in a circle and observe the response of the accelerometer; this experiment would directly relate to the centrifugal acceleration that occurs when a car or aircraft executes a turn.

13. Sample answer: Acceleration indicates how fast velocity is changing.

S.T.E.M. Lab continued

Answer Key for INDEPENDENT Inquiry

DEVELOP A PLAN

2. Accept all reasonable answers.

MAKE OBSERVATIONS

3. Sample answers are shown in the table below.

MOVEMENT OF STRING

While speeding up	While walking steadily	While slowing down
Rearward/positive	No change	Forward/negative

4. Sample answer: We observed positive acceleration when we moved faster and faster. We observed negative acceleration when we slowed our speed.

5. Sample answer: When we changed direction, we observed that the string moved in either a positive or negative way depending on the change we made.

ANALYZE THE RESULTS

6. Sample answer: Acceleration occurs whenever there is a change in speed or a change in direction.

7. Accept all reasonable answers. Students should observe the largest acceleration when they have the greatest change in speed.

8. Sample answer: Acceleration is a change in speed or direction over time and can be negative or positive.

Connect TO THE ESSENTIAL QUESTION

9. Answers will vary but should demonstrate comprehension of the accelerometer's purpose as well as its limitations, For example, students could spin in a circle and observe the response of the accelerometer; this experiment would directly relate to the centrifugal acceleration that occurs when a car or aircraft executes a turn.

10. Sample answer: Acceleration indicates how fast velocity is changing.

Name ______________________ Class ______________ Date ______________

S.T.E.M. LAB GUIDED Inquiry

Investigate Acceleration

In this lab, you will explore how acceleration changes relative to the movement of an object by observing the behavior of an accelerometer as you move around.

OBJECTIVES

- Make an accelerometer and use it to observe circumstances that involve acceleration.
- Determine the types of circumstances that lead to positive acceleration and to negative acceleration.

MATERIALS

For each group

- cardboard
- glue
- scissors
- string
- washer

For each student

- safety goggles

PROCEDURE

MAKE OBSERVATIONS

1. Use the template shown in the diagram on the next page along with the other materials to construct an acceleration measuring tool. Poke a hole through the circle indicated on the template and thread a string through the hole. Tie the metal washer to the string so that the weight will hang vertically when the accelerometer is at rest.

2. Hold the tool in your right hand so that the string falls over the $0\ m/s^2$ mark. When you are at rest, what happens to the weight and string?

   ____

   ____

3. Move the tool in the direction of the arrow. Try to produce both positive and negative acceleration without changing the direction of motion. What did you observe? How can you have a negative acceleration?

   ____

   ____

   ____

   ____

S.T.E.M. Lab continued

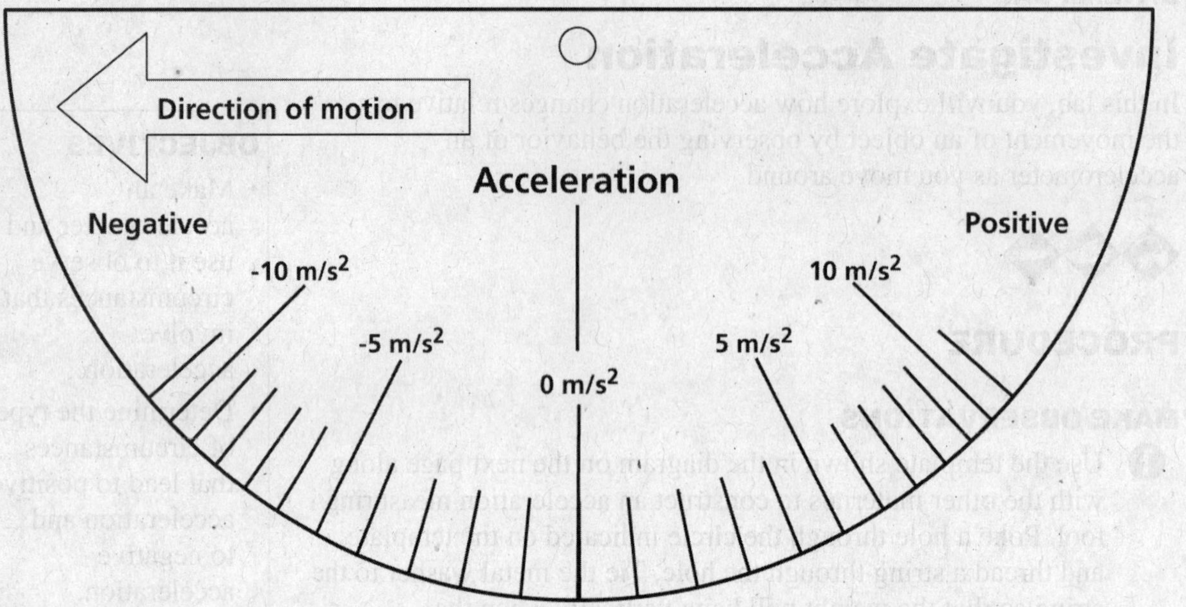

4 Try moving the tool backward. Record your observations below.

____

____

FORM A PREDICTION

5 Before you start to move, predict what will happen to the accelerometer when you walk forward very quickly increasing your speed for a few seconds, then walk steadily for another time period, and then slow down.

____

____

____

S.T.E.M. Lab continued

MAKE OBSERVATIONS

6. With the arrow pointing ahead of you, start to walk. Observe the motion of the string while you walk quickly. Record your observations in the table below.

MOVEMENT OF STRING

While speeding up	While walking steadily	While slowing down

7. Repeat Step 6, but this time observe the string while slowing down. Record your observations in the table.

8. Repeat Step 6 again, but observe the string while walking at a steady speed. Record your observations in the table.

ANALYZE THE RESULTS

9. Under what kinds of circumstances could you detect acceleration?

____

____

10. What was the largest acceleration (positive or negative) that you observed?

____

____

11. What do your observations indicate about acceleration?

____

____

Connect TO THE ESSENTIAL QUESTION

⑫ Can you think of any other tests to perform with the accelerometer?

____

____

⑬ In your own words, explain how velocity and acceleration are related.

____

____

Name ______________________ Class ______________ Date ______________________

S.T.E.M. LAB INDEPENDENT *Inquiry*

Investigate Acceleration

In this lab, you will explore how acceleration changes relative to the movement of an object by observing the behavior of an accelerometer as you move around.

OBJECTIVES

- Make an accelerometer and use it to observe circumstances that involve acceleration.
- Determine the types of circumstances that lead to positive acceleration and to negative acceleration.

MATERIALS

For each group
- cardboard
- glue
- scissors
- string
- washer

For each student
- safety goggles

PROCEDURE

MAKE OBSERVATIONS

1. Use the template shown in the diagram on the next page along with the other materials to construct an acceleration measuring tool. Poke a hole through the circle indicated on the template and thread a string through the hole. Tie the metal washer to the string so that the weight will hang vertically when the accelerometer is at rest.

DEVELOP A PLAN

2. Work together as a team to develop an experiment that allows you to find out information about the nature of acceleration using the tool you just made. Be sure that your experiments include ways to produce both positive and negative acceleration. Also be sure that your experiments include ways to test changing directions on acceleration. Write your plan below.

____

____

____

____

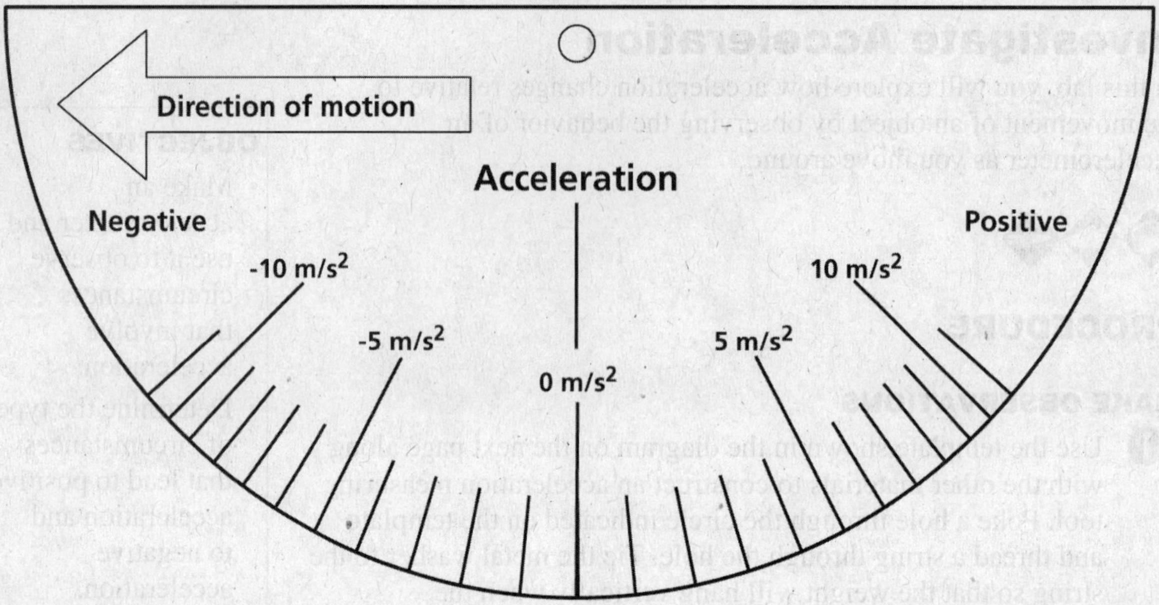

MAKE OBSERVATIONS

3 Ask your teacher to approve your plan and then carry it out. Record your observations below.

4 How were you able to demonstrate positive acceleration? Negative acceleration?

____

____

____

S.T.E.M. Lab continued

5 How were you able to demonstrate the effects of changing direction on acceleration?

ANALYZE THE RESULTS

6 Under what kinds of circumstances could you detect acceleration?

7 What was the largest acceleration (positive or negative) that you observed?

8 What do your observations indicate about acceleration?

Connect TO THE ESSENTIAL QUESTION

9 Can you think of any other tests to perform with the accelerometer?

10 In your own words, explain how velocity and acceleration are related.

QUICK LAB INDEPENDENT *Inquiry*

Net Force GENERAL

Small groups
20 minutes

LAB RATINGS LESS ← → MORE

Teacher Prep — 1
Student Setup — 2
Cleanup — 2

MATERIALS

For each group
- materials for investigation (see notes)
- scale, spring

For each student
- lab apron
- safety goggles

SAFETY INFORMATION

Remind students to review all safety cautions and icons before beginning this lab. Students may choose to investigate forces by dropping, pushing, or rolling objects. For such procedures, instruct them to use materials that will not easily break.

My Notes

TEACHER NOTES

In this activity, students will investigate the effect of balanced and unbalanced forces on objects. Give each group of students a spring scale and review how to use it with the class.

Then have students choose materials and devise a procedure to carry out their investigation. For example, students may observe the force due to gravity on an object by using a string to suspend it from a spring scale, noting that an equal and opposite upward force keeps the object still in the air. Students may then unbalance the forces on the object by eliminating the upward force by cutting the spring and releasing it from the spring scale, observing its direction of motion.

Make sure you have different types of materials available for students to use in their investigations in addition to the spring scale. These materials may include modeling clay, rubber balls, string, water, graduated cylinders, and beakers (for observing buoyant force).

Tip To help students visualize and understand forces, show them how to draw free-body diagrams. Students can use these diagrams to record their observations in this lab.

Student Tip Remember that the weight of an object is the force of gravity on that object.

Skills Focus Devising Procedures, Drawing Conclusions

Quick Lab continued

MODIFICATION FOR DIRECTED Inquiry

Give students a procedure for investigating buoyant force and force due to gravity. First, have students attach a ball of modeling clay to a string. Instruct students to hang the clay on a spring scale and record its weight. Then have students lower the clay into a beaker of water and record its weight. Ask students to find the difference between the readings on the spring scale to calculate the buoyant force on the submerged clay. Finally, have students release the clay from the spring scale in the beaker and observe the direction in which the clay moves. Students should explain how the net force determines the direction of motion of the clay.

Answer Key

1. Accept all reasonable answers.
2. Accept all reasonable answers.
   Teacher Prompt What are some forces that can act on your object? How can you balance these forces? How can you make the forces unequal?
3. Accept all reasonable answers.
4. Sample answer: When the forces were balanced, the object stayed in one place. The net force was zero.
   Teacher Prompt Equal forces acting in opposite directions are like opposite numbers. What happens when you add opposite numbers (such as 5 and -5)?
5. When the forces were unbalanced, the object moved in the direction of the net force.
   Teacher Prompt Which force on the object was the greatest? Did this force influence the motion of the object?

Name ______________________ Class ______________ Date ________________

QUICK LAB INDEPENDENT *Inquiry*

Net Force

In this lab, you will investigate the effect of balanced and unbalanced forces on an object. You will also consider how net force determines the object's direction of motion. Remember that the net force on an object is the combination of all the forces acting on the object.

OBJECTIVES

- Compare the effect of balanced and unbalanced forces on an object.
- Use net force to determine an object's direction of motion.

MATERIALS

For each group
- materials for investigation
- scale, spring

For each student
- lab apron
- safety goggles

PROCEDURE

1. In this lab, you will investigate the following question: What is the effect of balanced and unbalanced forces on an object? Write any thoughts you have about the question below.

____

____

____

____

2. With your group members, devise a procedure to investigate the question above. Write your procedure below.

____

____

____

____

____

____

____

____

Quick Lab continued

3. With teacher approval, carry out your procedure. Record your observations in the space below.

4. What happened when the forces on the object were balanced? What was the net force in this situation?

____

____

____

____

5. What happened when the forces on the object were unbalanced?

____

____

____

____

QUICK LAB DIRECTED Inquiry

First Law of Skateboarding GENERAL

Student pairs
15 minutes

LAB RATINGS

LESS ← → MORE

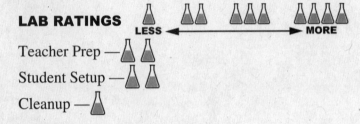

Teacher Prep — 2
Student Setup — 2
Cleanup — 1

MATERIALS

For each pair
- doll, rigid-body type
- skateboard

For each student
- safety goggles

My Notes

SAFETY INFORMATION

Remind students to review all safety cautions and icons before beginning this lab. Warn students to be careful when they push the skateboard. Do not allow students to sit, stand, or ride on the skateboards.

TEACHER NOTES

In this activity, students will explore the effects of balanced and unbalanced forces on the motion of an object. Have students bring in their own skateboards. Ballistics carts and janitor dollies are acceptable substitutes for a skateboard. Dolls should have a rigid body—stuffed dolls or stuffed animals will not work in this activity.

If time permits, have students explore how the effect of an applied force changes as the mass of an object changes. Students can change the mass of the doll by attaching washers or coins to the doll and repeating the experiment.

Skills Focus Making Observations, Applying Concepts

MODIFICATION FOR INDEPENDENT Inquiry

Have students investigate the meaning of inertia and brainstorm ways of modeling the effect of inertia on an object. Students should write procedures and a list of materials for any experiments they would like to conduct. Allow students to perform all reasonable experiments.

Answer Key

2. Sample answer: The doll falls over backward when the skateboard starts moving.

4. Sample answer: The doll falls over forward when the skateboard stops moving.

5. Sample answer: The doll was not moving. When a force was applied to the skateboard but not to the doll, the doll continued to not move, but the skateboard did move, so the doll fell over in a direction opposite the direction of the skateboard's motion.

6. Sample answer: The doll was moving with the skateboard. When a force was applied to the skateboard but not to the doll, the skateboard stopped moving but the doll kept moving, so the doll fell over in the direction of its motion.

QUICK LAB DIRECTED Inquiry

First Law of Skateboarding

In this lab, you will explore the effects of balanced and unbalanced forces on an object. You will apply forces to a skateboard and observe the effect these forces have on a doll traveling on top of the skateboard.

OBJECTIVE

- Investigate and describe how an unbalanced force acting on an object changes its speed, direction, and motion.

MATERIALS

For each pair

- doll, rigid-body type
- skateboard

For each student

- safety goggles

PROCEDURE

1. Place a **doll** in a seated position on the center of the skateboard.

2. Have your partner sit on the floor about 3 meters away from you. Give the skateboard a quick, firm push toward your partner. What happens to the doll as the skateboard moves toward your partner?

   ____

   ____

   ____

   ____

   ____

   ____

   ____

3. Practice pushing the skateboard as quickly and smoothly as you can, so that the doll travels from you to your partner without falling.

4. Push the skateboard smoothly toward your partner (as practiced in Step 3). Have your partner stop the skateboard suddenly, without making contact with the doll. What happens to the doll when your partner stops the skateboard?

   ____

   ____

   ____

   ____

   ____

   ____

   ____

Quick Lab continued

5 Newton's first law of motion states that objects in motion tend to stay in motion unless a force acts on the object. How does this law explain your observations from Step 2?

6 How does Newton's first law of motion explain your observations from Step 4?

S.T.E.M. LAB GUIDED *Inquiry* **AND** INDEPENDENT *Inquiry*

Newton's Laws of Motion GENERAL

Small groups

Two 45-minute class periods

LAB RATINGS

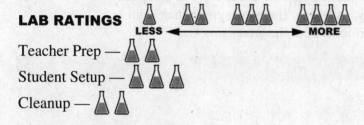

LESS ⟷ MORE

Teacher Prep — 2

Student Setup — 3

Cleanup — 2

MATERIALS

For each group

- bottle, plastic
- clay, modeling
- meterstick
- paper, construction
- scissors
- straws, one wider than the other (2)
- tape

For each student

- lab apron
- safety goggles

SAFETY INFORMATION

Remind students to review all safety cautions and icons before beginning this lab. Emphasize that students should always wear goggles when working with their rockets and to point projectiles away from other students. For the independent inquiry, instruct students to design rockets and launchers that are as safe as possible. The devices should not include any sharp objects.

TEACHER NOTES

In this lab, students will build a straw and bottle rocket to investigate Newton's Laws of Motion. In the first part of the lab, students will construct the rocket and launcher and record the rocket's flight distances. In the second part of the lab, students will modify the rocket or launcher to try to make the rocket fly farther. For the independent inquiry, students will design their own rocket launchers. Have materials such as straws, plastic bottles of various sizes, clay, and balloons available for students to choose from. To allow students more time to investigate, you may cut the paper strips in advance and give them to students on the day of the lab. Provide extra plastic bottles in case cracks develop from squeezing.

For best results, remind students to measure the rocket's flight distance consistently. For example, always measure from the launching point (tip of the straw) to the place where the rocket lands (tip of the straw). Either move all of the desks/tables in the room off to the side or locate a large open area on the school grounds (cafeteria, gymnasium, field, etc.) where the activity can be conducted without interference.

Tip This lab is designed to help students understand Newton's Second and Third Laws of Motion.

Student Tip Read through the procedure at least once before beginning your investigation so that you know how the finished rocket will look and function.

Skills Focus Forming Hypotheses, Making Tables, Applying Concepts

My Notes

S.T.E.M. Lab continued

MODIFICATION FOR DIRECTED Inquiry

Before beginning the lab, review Newton's Laws of Motion with students. Have them describe each law in their own words. Have small groups follow the procedure below to construct the rocket and launcher. As a class, develop a table in which students can record data. For Part II of the lab, assign each group a specific modification for their rocket. For example, one group may try using a larger plastic bottle for launching, one group may try using a straw with smaller mass or less clay, and so on. Have each group share with the class how the modification affected the performance of the group's rocket.

Answer Key for GUIDED Inquiry

MAKE OBSERVATIONS

6. Accept all reasonable answers.

DRAW CONCLUSIONS

7. Newton's first law: The unbalanced force of the air pushing on the straw changes the straw's motion. Newton's second law: The acceleration of the straw depends on the mass of the straw and how much force is applied to the launcher. Newton's third law: As the straw forces air backward, air forces the straw forward.
Teacher Prompt Are forces balanced or unbalanced when you launch the rocket? How do you know? What factors influence the acceleration of the straw? Can you identify any force pairs?

8. You would need to know the mass of the straw and the amount of force applied to it.
Teacher Prompt What factors influence the acceleration of the straw? What other variables are part of the equation F=ma?

FORM A HYPOTHESIS

9. Accept all reasonable answers.
Teacher Prompt How could you increase the force applied to the rocket? How could you decrease the mass of the rocket?

TEST THE HYPOTHESIS

11. Accept all reasonable answers.

ANALYZE THE RESULTS

12. Accept all reasonable answers.

13. Accept all reasonable answers.

14. Possible limits and errors include inconsistent force, inconsistent measurements, and changing more than one variable.

S.T.E.M. Lab continued

DRAW CONCLUSIONS

15. Accept all reasonable answers.
Teacher Prompt Think about the change you made to your rocket. Did this change affect the amount of force on your rocket? Did it affect the mass of your device?

16. Sample answer: rowing a boat or using a bow and arrow
Teacher Prompt What are some devices that use action and reaction forces? What machines have parts that you push or pull?

Connect TO THE ESSENTIAL QUESTION

17. The unbalanced force of the air pushing on the rocket caused it to launch. The force of gravity pulling downward brought the rocket to rest on the floor.
Teacher Prompt What causes an object to accelerate? Were forces on your rocket balanced or unbalanced? Why did your rocket gradually move toward the floor?

Answer Key for INDEPENDENT Inquiry

BUILD A MODEL

2. Accept all reasonable answers.

3. Accept all reasonable answers.

MAKE OBSERVATIONS

5. Accept all reasonable answers.

6. Accept all reasonable answers.

DRAW CONCLUSIONS

7. Newton's first law: The unbalanced force of the air pushing on the straw changes the straw's motion. Newton's second law: The acceleration of the straw depends on the mass of the straw and how much force is applied to the launcher. Newton's third law: As the straw forces air backward, air forces the straw forward.
Teacher Prompt Are forces balanced or unbalanced when you launch the rocket? How do you know? What factors influence the acceleration of the straw? Can you identify any force pairs?

8. You would need to know the mass of the straw and the amount of force applied to it.
Teacher Prompt What factors influence the acceleration of the straw? What other variables are part of the equation $F=ma$?

FORM A HYPOTHESIS

9. Accept all reasonable answers.

TEST THE HYPOTHESIS

11. Accept all reasonable answers.

S.T.E.M. Lab continued

ANALYZE THE RESULTS

12. Sample answer: Find the average flight distance for each rocket by dividing the sum of the distances by the total number of trials.

13. Accept all reasonable answers.

14. Possible limits and errors include inconsistent force, inconsistent measurements, and changing more than one variable.

DRAW CONCLUSIONS

15. Accept all reasonable answers.
Teacher Prompt Think about the change you made to your rocket. Did this change affect the amount of force on your rocket? Did it affect the mass of your device?

16. Sample answer: rowing a boat or using a bow and arrow
Teacher Prompt What are some devices that use action and reaction forces? What machines have parts that you push or pull?

Connect TO THE ESSENTIAL QUESTION

17. The unbalanced force of the air pushing on the rocket caused it to launch. The force of gravity pulling downward brought the rocket to rest on the floor.
Teacher Prompt What causes an object to accelerate? Were forces on your rocket balanced or unbalanced? Why did your rocket gradually move toward the floor?

Name ______________________ Class ____________ Date ______________

S.T.E.M. LAB GUIDED Inquiry

Newton's Laws of Motion

In this lab, you will build a straw and bottle rocket to investigate Newton's Laws of Motion. You will then apply your knowledge of Newton's Laws to modify your rocket to try and make it fly farther. Newton's Second and Third Laws will be especially important in this activity. According to Newton's Second Law, the acceleration of an object depends on the mass of the object and how much force is applied. Newton's Third Law states that all forces act in pairs. When one object applies a force to a second object, the second object applies a force to the first object that is equal in size and opposite in direction.

OBJECTIVES

- Describe the relationships among force, mass, and acceleration.
- Explain how forces act in pairs.

MATERIALS

For each group
- bottle, plastic
- clay, modeling
- meterstick
- paper, construction
- scissors
- straws, one wider than the other (2)
- tape

For each student
- lab apron
- safety goggles

PROCEDURE

Part I

BUILD A MODEL

1. To build the rocket launcher, place the narrow straw into the bottle so that it is half in and half out. Seal the top of the bottle by placing clay firmly around the straw.

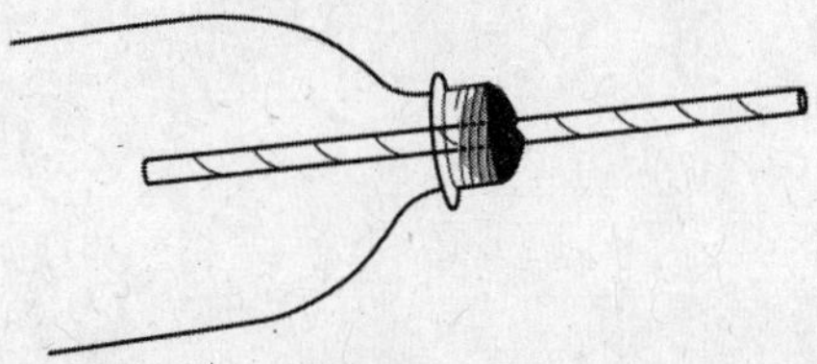

2. To build the rocket, cut two strips of paper, 8 cm and 10 cm long, and about 2 cm wide. Use tape to make each strip into a loop. Tape both loops to the wide straw, one at each end. Put a small ball of clay into the end of the straw near the smaller loop.

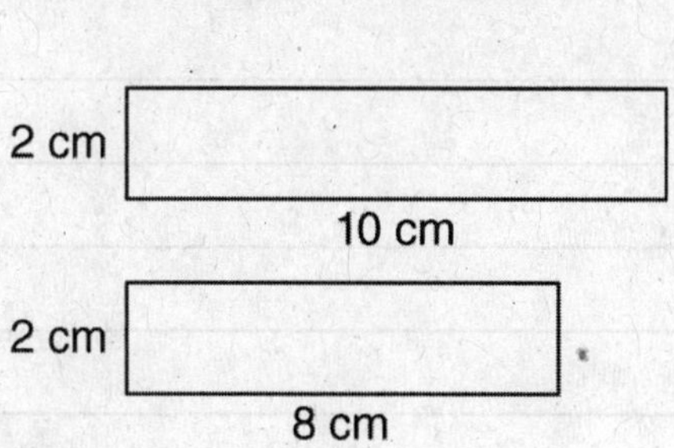

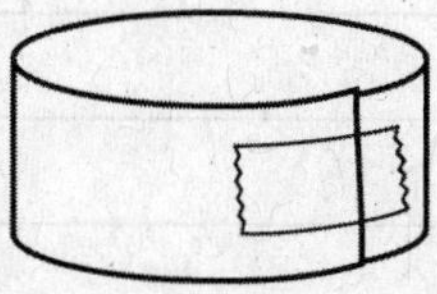

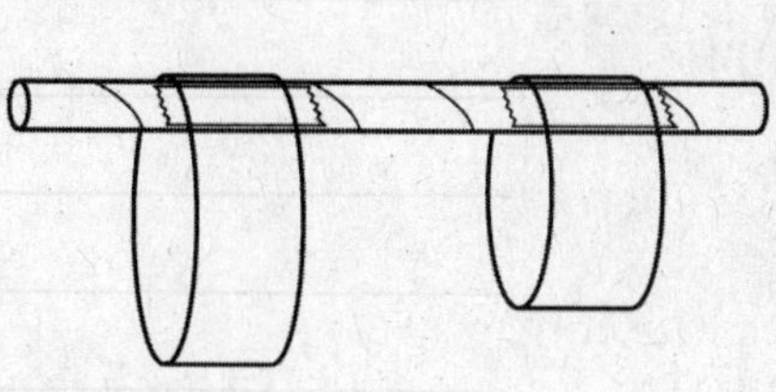

S.T.E.M. Lab continued

3. Set up the rocket and launcher. Slide the rocket-straw onto the launcher-straw. Position the bottle at the edge of a table so that the straws hang over. Place a meter stick on the floor with one end at the edge of the table.

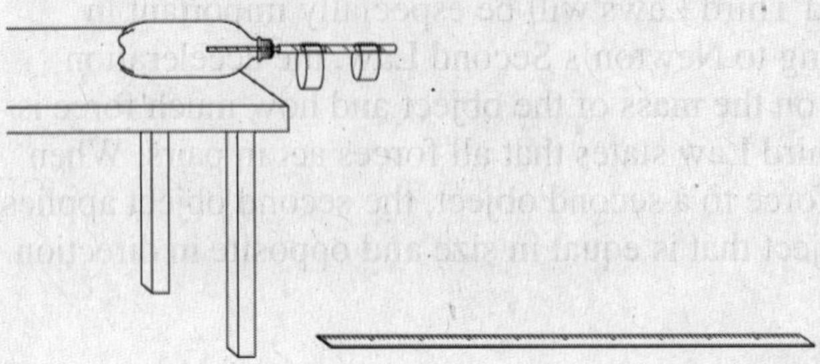

MAKE OBSERVATIONS

4. Test your model by squeezing the bottle to launch the rocket. To find the flight distance, measure the distance from the edge of the table to the landing point (the point on the straw closest to the launcher).

5. Launch the rocket four times, squeezing the bottle the same way each time. Measure the distance the rocket flies in each trial.

6. Make a table to show the data collected during your investigation.

DRAW CONCLUSIONS

7. **Applying Concepts** Use Newton's Laws to explain why the rocket flies.

____

____

____

____

____

____

8 **Identifying Data** What information would you need to calculate the acceleration of the straw rocket? Hint: Newton's Second Law can be expressed mathematically as F=ma.

Part II

FORM A HYPOTHESIS

9 Think of a change you could make to your device to make the rocket fly farther. Form a hypothesis that explains how this change will make your rocket fly farther.

TEST THE HYPOTHESIS

10 With teacher approval, modify your rocket according to your hypothesis.

11 Launch your modified rocket four times, measuring the flight distance for each trial. Create a data table below in which to record your results.

ANALYZE THE RESULTS

12 **Analyzing Data** Calculate the average flight distance for each rocket. (Divide the sum of the distances by the number of trials.) Which rocket had the greatest average distance?

13. **Evaluating Hypotheses** Compare your results with your hypothesis. Do your results support your hypothesis?

____

____

____

____

14. **Describing Constraints** What limits or errors could have happened in your experiment?

____

____

____

DRAW CONCLUSIONS

15. **Applying Concepts** How do Newton's Laws of Motion explain the performance of your modified rocket?

____

____

____

____

____

____

16. **Recognizing Concepts** In what other real-life devices can you observe Newton's Laws?

____

____

____

____

Connect TO THE ESSENTIAL QUESTION

17. **Explaining Events** What caused your rocket to start moving? What brought it to rest?

____

____

____

____

Name ______________________ Class ____________ Date ________________

S.T.E.M. LAB INDEPENDENT *Inquiry*

Newton's Laws of Motion

In this lab, you will build a straw and bottle rocket to investigate Newton's Laws of Motion. You will then apply your knowledge of Newton's Laws to modify your rocket to make it fly farther. Newton's Second and Third Laws will be especially important in this activity. According to Newton's Second Law, the acceleration of an object depends on the mass of the object and how much force is applied. Newton's Third Law states that all forces act in pairs. When one object applies a force to a second object, the second object applies a force to the first object that is equal in size and opposite in direction.

OBJECTIVES

- Describe the relationships among force, mass, and acceleration.
- Explain how forces act in pairs.

MATERIALS

For each group
- bottle, plastic
- clay, modeling
- meterstick
- paper, construction
- scissors
- straws, one wider than the other (2)
- tape

For each student
- lab apron
- safety goggles

PROCEDURE

Part I

BUILD A MODEL

1. To build the rocket, cut two strips of paper, 8 cm and 10 cm long, and about 2 cm wide. Use tape to make each strip into a loop. Tape both loops to the wide straw, one at each end. Put a small ball of clay into the end of the straw near the smaller loop.

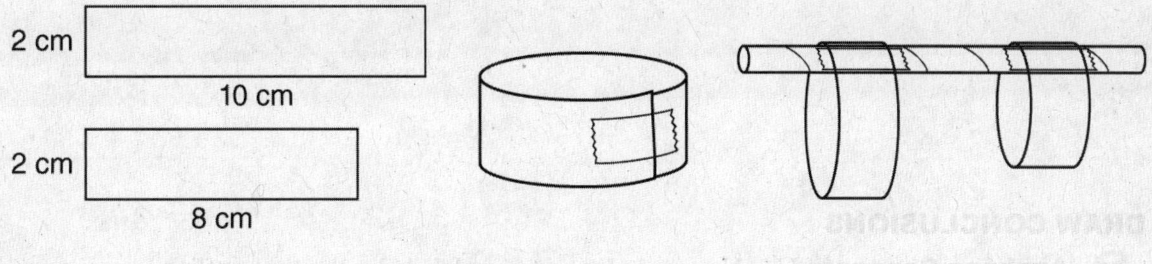

2. What materials could you use to build a launcher for the rocket?

____

____

____

____

S.T.E.M. Lab continued

3. Describe how you plan to build the rocket launcher.

4. With teacher approval, build your device. Test your rocket to make sure it works as you expected.

MAKE OBSERVATIONS

5. Devise a procedure that will allow you to collect data about the flight distance of your rocket.

6. Make a table to show the data collected during your investigation.

DRAW CONCLUSIONS

7. **Applying Concepts** Use Newton's Laws to explain why the rocket flies.

8 **Identifying Data** What information would you need to calculate the acceleration of the straw rocket? Hint: Newton's Second Law can be expressed mathematically as F=ma.

____

____

Part II

FORM A HYPOTHESIS

9 Think of a change you could make to your device to make the rocket fly farther. Form a hypothesis that explains how this change will make your rocket fly farther.

____

____

____

TEST THE HYPOTHESIS

10 With teacher approval, modify your rocket according to your hypothesis.

11 Collect data using your procedure from Part I of the lab. Make a table below to show the results of your investigation.

ANALYZE THE RESULTS

12 **Analyzing Data** How can you compare the performance of your original and modified rockets?

____

____

____

____

S.T.E.M. Lab continued

13 **Evaluating Hypotheses** Do your results support your hypothesis?

14 **Describing Constraints** What limits or errors could have happened in your experiment?

DRAW CONCLUSIONS

15 **Applying Concepts** How do Newton's Laws of Motion explain the performance of your modified rocket?

16 **Recognizing Concepts** In what other real-life devices can you observe Newton's Laws?

Connect TO THE ESSENTIAL QUESTION

17 **Explaining Events** What caused your rocket to start moving? What brought it to rest?

QUICK LAB DIRECTED *Inquiry*

Falling Water BASIC

Small groups
20 minutes

LAB RATINGS

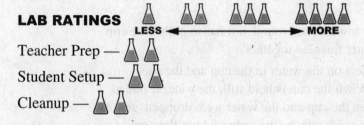

LESS ← → MORE

Teacher Prep — 2
Student Setup — 2
Cleanup — 2

MATERIALS

For each group
- cup, paper
- paper towels
- scissors
- tub, plastic
- water

For each student
- lab apron
- safety goggles

SAFETY INFORMATION

Remind students to review all safety cautions and icons before beginning this lab. Scissors are sharp and should be handled with care. Spilled water can be a slipping hazard and should be cleaned up immediately.

TEACHER NOTES

In this activity, students will observe how objects in free fall accelerate at the same rate by comparing the effect gravity has on water flowing through a hole in a stationary cup to the effect gravity has on water flowing through a hole in a cup in free fall.

Food coloring may be added to the water so that students will see the water better. If possible, the activity can be done outdoors to minimize cleanup. Students should be instructed to half-fill the cups with water, to reduce the mess. To prevent slipping, spread plenty of newspapers on the floor.

Tip This activity may help students better understand the relationship between gravity and falling objects.

Skills Focus Making Observations, Drawing Conclusions

My Notes

MODIFICATION FOR GUIDED *Inquiry*

Provide students with a list of materials, and have students brainstorm experiments that would demonstrate the effect of gravity on falling water. Students should write up a list of procedures and should develop a hypothesis for what they expect to happen in their experiment. Allow students to proceed with all reasonable experiments.

Quick Lab continued

Answer Key

4. Sample answer: Water is falling through the hole in the cup into the tub.

6. Sample answer: The water and the cup fall into the tub, but there is no water flowing through the hole in the cup.

8. Sample answer: Gravity caused the water to flow through the hole in the cup and accelerate toward the ground.

9. Sample answer: Gravity pulled the water toward the ground, but it also pulled the cup toward the ground, so the cup and the water traveled together.

10. Sample answer: Gravity has the same affect on the water in the cup and the cup itself—it pulls both toward the ground. When the cup is held still, the water is pulled toward the ground through the hole. When the cup and the water were dropped, gravity accelerated both toward the ground at the same rate, so the water did not flow out of the hole.

Name ______________________ Class ______________ Date ______________

QUICK LAB DIRECTED Inquiry

Falling Water

In this lab, you will observe the effect that gravity has on falling objects.

OBJECTIVES

- Investigate how gravity affects objects close to the earth.
- Describe the gravitational force.

MATERIALS

For each group
- cup, paper
- paper towels
- scissors
- tub, plastic
- water

For each student
- lab apron
- safety goggles

PROCEDURE

1. Place a **wide plastic tub** on the floor.
2. Take a **paper cup** and punch a small hole in the side, near the bottom.
3. Hold your finger over the hole, and half-fill the cup with **water**. Keep your finger over the hole. Hold the cup 2–3 feet above the tub.
4. Remove your finger from the hole. Record your observations below.

____

____

____

____

____

5. Cover the hole, and half-fill the cup with water.
6. Uncover the hole and drop the cup at the same time. Record your observations below.

____

____

____

____

____

7. Clean up any spilled water with **paper towels**.

Quick Lab continued

8 How did gravity affect the water in the cup in Step 4?

____

____

____

____

____

____

____

9 How did gravity affect the water in the cup in Step 6?

____

____

____

____

____

____

____

10 Why didn't water flow through the hole in the cup in Step 6?

____

____

____

____

____

____

____

____

____

QUICK LAB DIRECTED *Inquiry*

Gravity and Distance GENERAL

Student pairs
20 minutes

MATERIALS
For each pair
- no materials

My Notes

LAB RATINGS

LESS ⟷ MORE

Teacher Prep — 1
Student Setup — 1
Cleanup — 1

SAFETY INFORMATION

Remind students to review all safety cautions and icons before beginning this lab.

TEACHER NOTES

In this activity, students will determine the relationship between the mass of an object and the magnitude of an object's gravitational force.

The gravitational force between two objects is described by this formula:

$$g = \frac{GMm}{r^2}$$

In this formula, g is the force of gravity, G is the gravitational constant, M is the mass of the first object, m is the mass of the second object, and r is the distance between the two objects. As the equation shows, when you increase the distance between two objects, the gravitational force between the two objects decreases.

In a simplified version of the equation, the gravitational constant is dropped and the force of gravity between two objects is calculated in terms of a proportionality, or a unit-less number. For example, Venus is at a distance of 0.3 AU from Earth and has a mass 0.8 times Earth's. The gravity force of Venus upon Earth is:

$$g = \frac{(0.8)(1.0)}{(0.3)^2} = 8.9$$

Skills Focus Performing Calculations, Explaining Results

MODIFICATION FOR INDEPENDENT *Inquiry*

Have students research the gravitational forces exerted by various objects in the solar system. Students should use the information they find to determine the relationship between the mass of an object, distance from that object, and the gravitational force exerted by that object. Students should be encouraged to summarize their findings in a chart and, time permitting, to write an algebraic equation that generalizes their findings to all objects in the solar system.

Quick Lab continued

Answer Key

1. Sample answer:

Planet	Distance (AU)	Mass (Earths)	Force (units)
Venus	0.3	0.8	8.9
Mars	0.5	0.1	0.4
Jupiter	4.2	317	17.9
Saturn	8.5	95	1.3
Uranus	18.0	14	0.04

2. Sample answer: Venus, because its gravitational force is 8.9 units, while that of Mars is only 0.4 units.

3. Sample answer: The gravitational force between Earth and Venus (8.9 units) is nearly the same as between Earth and Saturn (1.3) because, although Saturn is much farther away (8.5 AU versus 0.3 AU), it is much more massive than Venus (8.5 Earth masses compared to Venus that has a mass equivalent to 0.8 Earth's mass).

4. Sample answer: Jupiter is at a distance of 4.2 AU from Earth, and Saturn is at 8.5 AU, so they are 8.5 – 4.2 = 4.3 AU apart. Jupiter–Saturn = 317 × 95/(4.3 × 4.3) = 1,628 units. Mars is 4.2 – 0.5 = 3.7 AU from Jupiter, so Mars–Jupiter = 317 × 0.1/(3.7 × 3.7) = 2.3 units. So, Saturn has the strongest gravitational force acting on Jupiter.

Name ________________________ Class ________________ Date ________________

QUICK LAB DIRECTED Inquiry

Gravity and Distance

In this lab, you will use the information given in the table to determine the relationship between the gravitational force between two objects, the distance between two objects, and the mass of each object.

OBJECTIVES

- Investigate and describe the force of gravity.
- Explore the law of gravity by recognizing that every object exerts gravitational force on every other object.
- Describe the relationship between the distance between two objects and the gravitational force they exert on each other.

MATERIALS

For each pair

- no materials

PROCEDURE

1 Complete the table by calculating the gravitational force each planet exerts on Earth (Earth's mass = 1.0), according to this equation:

$$g = \frac{M_{earth} M_{planet}}{d^2}$$

Planet	Distance (AU)	Mass Planet (Earths)	Force (units)
Venus	0.3	0.8	8.9
Mars	0.5	0.1	
Jupiter	4.2	317	
Saturn	8.5	95	
Uranus	18.0	14	

2 Which nearby planet affects Earth the most? Explain.

____

____

____

____

____

____

____

Quick Lab continued

3 Why is the gravitational force between Earth and Venus very close to the gravitational force between Earth and Jupiter, even though Jupiter is much farther from Earth than Venus is?

____

____

____

____

____

____

____

4 Which pair of planets exerts the strongest gravitational force, Saturn and Jupiter, or Mars and Jupiter? Explain your answer in the space below.

____

____

____

____

____

____

____

QUICK LAB DIRECTED Inquiry

Free-Fall Distances GENERAL

Student pairs
20 minutes

MATERIALS
For each pair
- graph paper (optional)

LAB RATINGS

LESS ← → MORE

Teacher Prep — 1
Student Setup — 1
Cleanup — 1

My Notes

SAFETY INFORMATION

Remind students to review all safety cautions and icons before beginning this lab.

TEACHER NOTES

In this activity, students will analyze information about free fall times on different planets to determine the relationship between a planet's gravitational force and the speed of an object in free fall.

Tip This activity may help students better understand the relationship between gravitational force and the amount of time an object spends in free fall.

Skills Focus Interpreting Tables, Constructing Graphs, Performing Calculations

MODIFICATION FOR GUIDED Inquiry

Have students research the relationship between gravity and the time spent in free fall on Earth and on other planets. Students should use the information they find to create a graph that describes the differences in free fall times on three different planets. This graph can be used to answer the questions in the lab.

Quick Lab continued

Answer Key

1. Sample answer: Earth, because for every time interval, the free fall distance is the largest, so the acceleration of gravity is the largest for this body
2. Sample answer:

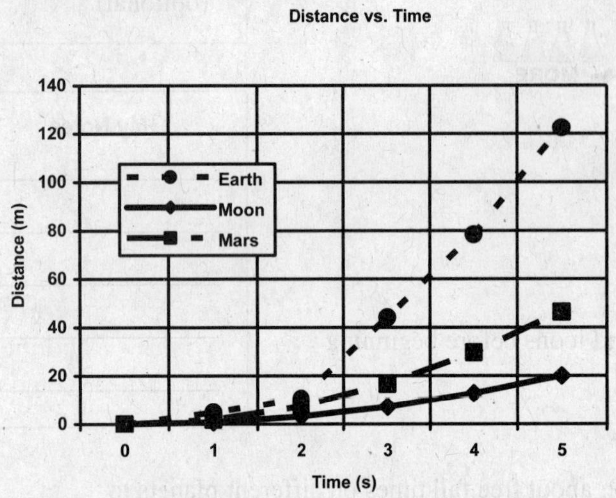

3. Sample answer: about 1 second, according to the table
4. Sample answer: The nearest table entry is for 12.8 meters, which takes 4 seconds, so the astronaut has about 4 seconds.
5. Sample answer: $T = 41$ seconds

Name ______________________________ Class __________________ Date ____________________

QUICK LAB DIRECTED *Inquiry*

Free-Fall Distances

In this lab, you will determine the relationship between gravity and distance traveled during free fall by analyzing free fall data from three different planets.

OBJECTIVES

- Graph the relationship between distance traveled in free fall and time spent in free fall for three different planets.
- Interpret the relationship between the force of gravity and the distance traveled per unit time for an object moving at a constant speed on different planets.

MATERIALS

For each pair

- graph paper (optional)

PROCEDURE

1. According to the data table, which planet has the strongest gravitational field? Explain your answer.

Distance Traveled in Free Fall on Three Planets

Time (s)	Earth (m)	Moon (m)	Mars (m)
1	4.9	0.8	1.9
2	19.6	3.2	7.4
3	44.1	7.2	16.7
4	78.4	12.8	29.6
5	122.5	20.0	46.3

____

____

____

____

____

2. In the space below or on graph paper, create a line graph of the distance traveled in free fall versus the time spent in free fall on Earth, Mars, and the moon.

Quick Lab continued

3 A 2-meter-tall astronaut standing on Mars drops her glasses from her nose. How long will it take the glasses to reach the ground? Show your calculations.

4 A clumsy astronaut falls into a crater on the moon. The crater is 13 meters deep. How long will the astronaut have before he hits the ground? Show your calculations.

5 The free fall distance for Earth is given by the formula $D = 4.9 \times T^2$, where D is distance in meters and T is time in seconds. How long would it take a package dropped from a plane flying at 8,300 meters (25,000 feet) to land on the ground? Show your calculations.

QUICK LAB DIRECTED Inquiry

Pressure Differences BASIC

Student pairs
20 minutes

LAB RATINGS LESS ⟷ MORE

Teacher Prep — 1
Student Setup — 2
Cleanup — 2

SAFETY INFORMATION

Remind students to review all safety cautions and icons before beginning this lab. Students should clean up any water that spills and should take care when working with food coloring to avoid staining clothes. Students should not share straws. Have paper towels available to clean up any spilled water.

TEACHER NOTES

In this activity, students will investigate how the speed of air affects air pressure. They will blow air across the open end of a straw placed in a cup of water, and make observations about what happens to the level of the water in the straw. They will use their observations to draw conclusions about the relationship between air speed and air pressure.

Tip Circulate as students are conducting their experiments to make sure they have their straws positioned correctly.

Student Tip Remember that when we speak about fluid pressure, both water and air are considered fluids because they can flow. Try to think of real-life examples of changes in fluid pressure.

Skills Focus Making Observations, Drawing Conclusions

MODIFICATION FOR GUIDED Inquiry

Provide students with the materials and the problem to investigate. The problem can be phrased as a question, such as, "How will differences in air pressure affect the way fluid flows?" Provide some oversight, but let students experiment on their own as to how to manipulate the materials to create differences in fluid pressure (both in the air and in the water in the straw).

MATERIALS

For each pair
- cup, clear plastic
- food coloring
- marker, permanent
- ruler, metric
- straws, clear (3)
- tape or small piece of clay
- water

For each student
- lab apron
- safety goggles

My Notes

Quick Lab continued

Answer Key

8. Sample data:

Sketch of two straws	Trial 1: Slower air speed	Trial 2: Faster air speed
Accept all reasonable answers.	Sample answer: The level of the water rose one centimeter on the straw.	Sample answer: The level of the water rose three centimeters on the straw.

9. Sample answer: When I blew into one straw, the water level rose in the other straw. The harder I blew, the more the water level rose.

10. Sample answer: Water rose higher in the straw as the air speed across the top increased.

11. Sample answer: As the speed of air moving across the top of the straw increased, the air pressure in the vertical straw decreased.
Teacher Prompt Think about what happened to the water in the straw when you increased the air speed across the top. How can you use changes in air pressure to account for this observation?

12. Sample answer: The wind causes a decrease in air pressure inside the box as it passes over. This decrease in air pressure results in movement of the paper.

QUICK LAB DIRECTED *Inquiry*

Pressure Differences

In this lab, you will investigate how differences in air speed affect air pressure. You will blow into one straw and watch how it changes the level of water in a second straw. You'll then work with your partner to draw a conclusion about how air flow rate affects air pressure.

OBJECTIVES

- Investigate how the speed of air movement affects fluid flow.
- Understand how pressure differences can cause fluids to flow from areas of relatively high pressure to areas of relatively low pressure.

MATERIALS

For each pair

- cup, clear plastic
- food coloring
- marker, permanent
- ruler, metric
- straws, clear (3)
- tape or small piece of clay
- water

For each student

- lab apron
- safety goggles

PROCEDURE

1. Use the marker and ruler to mark off 1 centimeter (cm) intervals along the length of one of the straws.
2. Half-fill the plastic cup with water.
3. Put 5 or 6 drops of food coloring into the water and stir it. Place the marked straw into the water and hold it upright so that the level of the water in the straw matches one of the marks on the straw. Don't let the straw rest on the bottom of the cup. Use a piece of tape to secure the straw to the cup.
4. Hold the other straw in a horizontal position. Line up the opening of the straws, so that when you blow into the horizontal straw, the air blows across the top of the vertical straw in the cup.

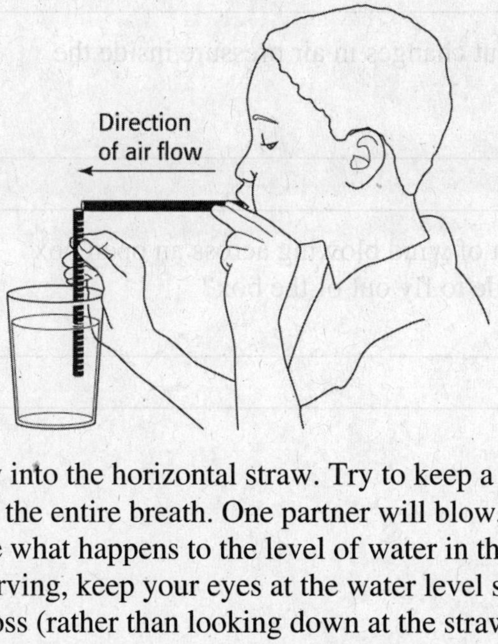

5. Blow gently into the horizontal straw. Try to keep a gentle and consistent air pressure for the entire breath. One partner will blow, and the other partner will observe what happens to the level of water in the vertical straw. If you're observing, keep your eyes at the water level so you're looking straight across (rather than looking down at the straw).
6. Blow again into the straw. This time, blow harder into the straw to increase the air speed. Try to keep the entire breath steady.

Quick Lab continued

7. Repeat the same process, this time switching partners. When you switch, use a new straw.

8. Record your observations in the table below.

WATER LEVEL OBSERVATIONS

Sketch of two straws	Trial 1: Slower air speed	Trial 2: Faster air speed

9. What happened to the water in the vertical straw as you blew?

____

____

10. Which way did the water in the vertical straw move when you increased the speed of blowing air?

____

____

11. What do your results suggest about changes in air pressure inside the vertical straw?

____

____

12. How does this explain why a gust of wind blowing across an open box causes a sheet of paper lying inside to fly out of the box?

____

____

QUICK LAB DIRECTED *Inquiry*

Finding the Buoyant Force GENERAL

Small groups

20 minutes

LAB RATINGS

LESS ⟵ ⟶ MORE

Teacher Prep — 2 flasks

Student Setup — 3 flasks

Cleanup — 2 flasks

MATERIALS

For each group

- clay, modeling
- graduated cylinder
- scale, spring
- string
- water

For each student

- gloves
- lab apron
- safety goggles

SAFETY INFORMATION

Remind students to review all safety cautions and icons before beginning this lab.

TEACHER NOTES

In this activity, students will calculate the buoyant force exerted by water on a ball of clay. Then, they will determine the relationship between the volume of water the ball of clay displaces and the buoyant force exerted by the water.

Skills Focus Practicing Lab Techniques, Performing Calculations, Drawing Conclusions

My Notes

MODIFICATION FOR GUIDED *Inquiry*

Have students determine a procedure for finding the relationship between water displacement and buoyant force. Allow students to proceed with all reasonable procedures.

Answer Key

1. Answers will vary.
2. Answers will vary.
3. Sample answer: The weight of the clay decreases as the clay enters the water.
4. Answers will vary.
5. Answers will vary.
6. Sample answer: When the clay enters the water, the water exerts a force against it in the direction opposite gravity, causing the scale to record a smaller value.
7. Answers will vary.
8. Answers will vary.
9. Sample answer: The buoyant force is equal to the weight of the clay when it is completely out of the water minus the weight of the clay when it is completely underwater.

Name ______________________________ Class __________________ Date ______________________

QUICK LAB DIRECTED Inquiry

Finding the Buoyant Force

In this lab, you will determine the relationship between buoyant force and water displacement by making force and volume measurements on a ball of clay before and after it is submerged in water.

OBJECTIVE

- Investigate and describe buoyant force.

MATERIALS

For each group

- clay, modeling
- graduated cylinder
- scale, spring
- string
- water

For each student

- gloves
- lab apron
- safety goggles

PROCEDURE

1. Use **string** to attach a ball of **modeling clay** to a **spring scale**. Record the weight of the clay in the space below.

   ____

2. Half fill a **graduated cylinder** with **water**. Record the volume of water in the space below.

   ____

3. Slowly lower the clay into the graduated cylinder. Do not let the spring scale get wet. How does the weight of the clay change as it enters the water?

   ____

4. When the clay is completely submerged in water, record its weight, according to the spring scale, in the space below.

   ____

5. While the clay remains completely submerged, record the new volume of the water in the graduated cylinder.

   ____

6. Explain why the reading on the spring scale changed as the clay entered the water.

   ____
   ____
   ____
   ____
   ____
   ____

7. Use the difference in the readings on the spring scale to calculate the buoyant force when the clay was completely underwater. Show your calculations in the space below.

8. How much water did the ball of clay displace? Record your answer in the space below.

9. How is the buoyant force that the water exerts on the clay related to the volume of water displaced by the clay?

FIELD LAB DIRECTED *Inquiry* **AND**

Pressure in Fluids GENERAL

Small groups

45 minutes

LAB RATINGS LESS ⟷ MORE

Teacher Prep — 2

Student Setup — 3

Cleanup — 2

SAFETY INFORMATION

Remind students to review all safety cautions and icons before beginning this lab. This lab must be conducted so that water flowing from the hole in the plastic bottle does not spill onto the floor and pose a safety hazard. If possible, conduct the lab outdoors where the water can seep into the ground. If this is not possible, provide each team with a bucket to collect the water that flows from the bottle. Tell students to wipe up any water that spills on the floor before moving on to the next step. Students should stand clear of the bottle to avoid becoming wet. Students should also use caution and wear hand protection and safety goggles when poking a nail through the plastic bottle. Have paper towels available to clean up spills.

MATERIALS

For each group

- bottle, large
- bottle, small
- can, coffee
- container, plastic
- funnel
- marker, permanent
- meterstick
- nail
- pencil, colored (2)
- ruler, metric
- water

For each student

- lab apron
- safety goggles

My Notes

____

____

____

____

____

TEACHER NOTES

In this activity, students will fill plastic bottles with water to certain levels. Any size bottles can be used as long as they are different sizes.The plastic bottles will have small holes punched in them. Students will cover the holes with a finger and then release the finger. When they do, water will squirt from the hole. Students will use a meterstick to measure the distance the water travels. They will repeat this process with different amounts of water and different sized bottles. Students will create or fill in data tables, then analyze the data to form hypotheses about the relationship between water pressure and water depth. If coffee cans are not available, a chair, stool, or any other type of stand can be used.

Tip Be sure to complete this lab in an outside area with plenty of space, as it's likely to get very wet. Even when completed outside, you may need a couple of towels to clean up wet materials or students.

Student Tip Try to follow the exact same procedures with the small and large bottles.

Skills Focus Creating Tables, Analyzing Data, Taking Measurements

MODIFICATION FOR INDEPENDENT *Inquiry*

Tell students that they will use the provided materials to investigate the relationship between water pressure and depth. Tell them that they will need to use both sizes of plastic bottles and to measure how far water can squirt from the bottles. Challenge them to devise procedures that use all of the materials and investigate the questions of the lab. Students should create their own data tables and analyze the data with limited or no teacher assistance.

Field Lab continued

Answer Key for DIRECTED Inquiry

FORM A PREDICTION

6. Sample answer: When my finger is lifted off the bottle, I think the water will squirt 30 centimeters (cm) away from the bottle.
Teacher Prompt How far do you think the water will squirt?

TEST THE PREDICTION

11. Sample answer:

DISTANCE WATER SQUIRTS WITH SMALL BOTTLE

Depth of water in small bottle (cm)	Trial 1	Trial 2	Trial 3	Average
12	14 cm	13 cm	12.5 cm	13.2 cm
11	12 cm	10.5 cm	14 cm	12.2 cm
10	11.5 cm	10 cm	10 cm	10.5 cm

12. Sample answer:

DISTANCE WATER SQUIRTS WITH LARGE BOTTLE

Depth of water in large bottle (cm)	Trial 1	Trial 2	Trial 3	Average
12	14.5 cm	13 cm	12.5 cm	13.3 cm
11	13 cm	12.5 cm	11.5 cm	12.3 cm
10	12.5 cm	9.5 cm	11.5 cm	11.2 cm

ANALYZE THE RESULTS

13. Accept all reasonable answers.
14. Sample answer: The depth of the water is greater when the bottle is more full.
15. Sample answer: The water traveled farther when the bottle was more full.
Teacher Prompt Think about why the water traveled farther when the bottle was more full.
16. Accept all reasonable answers.

DRAW CONCLUSIONS

17. Sample answer: If the depth of water is lowered, then the pressure will be lower because depth of water affects water pressure.
18. Sample answer: It's possible that the nails made holes of different sizes in each bottle.
19. Accept all reasonable answers. Students should understand that water pressure at the bottom of the dam is greater than water pressure at the top of the dam.
20. Accept all reasonable answers.

Field Lab continued

Connect TO THE ESSENTIAL QUESTION

21. Sample answer: The water pressure was slightly greater in the larger bottle because there was more water at the same depth.

Answer Key for GUIDED Inquiry

FORM A PREDICTION

6. Sample answer: When my finger is lifted off the bottle, I think the water will squirt 30 centimeters (cm) away from the bottle.
Teacher Prompt How far do you think the water will squirt?

TEST THE PREDICTION

12. Sample answer:
DISTANCE WATER SQUIRTS WITH SMALL BOTTLE

Depth of water in large bottle (cm)	Trial 1	Trial 2	Trial 3	Average
12	11.5 cm	12 cm	12 cm	11.8 cm
11	11 cm	12.5 cm	11.5 cm	11.7 cm
10	9.5 cm	9 cm	11 cm	9.8 cm

13. Sample answer:
DISTANCE WATER SQUIRTS WITH LARGE BOTTLE

Depth of water in small bottle (cm)	Trial 1	Trial 2	Trial 3	Average
12	14 cm	13 cm	15.5 cm	14.2 cm
11	12 cm	11.5 cm	14 cm	12.5 cm
10	11.5 cm	10.5 cm	10 cm	10.7 cm

ANALYZE THE RESULTS

14. Accept all reasonable answers.
15. Sample answer: The depth of the water is greater when the bottle is more full.
16. Sample answer: The water traveled farther when the bottle was more full.
Teacher Prompt Start to think about why the water traveled farther when the bottle was more full.
17. Accept all reasonable answers.

Field Lab continued

DRAW CONCLUSIONS

18. Sample answer: If the depth of water is lowered, then the pressure will be lower because depth of water affects water pressure.

19. Sample answer: It's possible that the nails made holes of different sizes in each bottle.

20. Accept all reasonable answers. Students should understand that water pressure at the bottom of the dam is greater than water pressure at the top of the dam.

21. Accept all reasonable answers.

Connect TO THE ESSENTIAL QUESTION

22. Sample answer: The water pressure was slightly greater in the larger bottle because there was more water at the same depth.

Name ______________________ Class ______________ Date ____________________

FIELD LAB DIRECTED Inquiry

Pressure in Fluids

In this lab, you will investigate the relationship between the depth of water and the pressure of water. You will poke a hole in plastic bottles, fill them with water, and measure how far water squirts out of the holes. You will fill in tables to display the data you collect. You'll then work with your group to form a hypothesis about water pressure and water depth.

OBJECTIVE

- Investigate the relationship between water pressure and water depth.

MATERIALS

For each group

- bottle, large
- bottle, small
- can, coffee
- container, plastic
- funnel
- marker, permanent
- meterstick
- nail
- pencil, colored (2)
- ruler, metric
- water

For each student

- lab apron
- safety goggles

PROCEDURE

BUILD A MODEL

1. Use a nail to carefully poke a hole in the side of each bottle. The hole should be close to the bottom of the bottle, as shown in the image below.

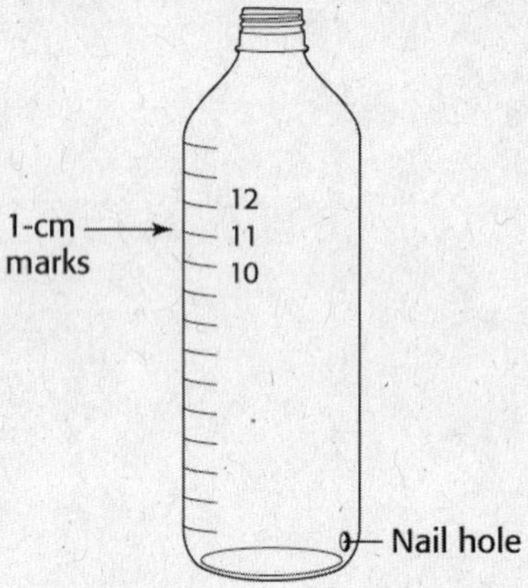

2. Use your ruler and permanent marker to mark off 1 centimenter (cm) increments on each bottle. Lower numbers should be at the bottom; start with 0 and go to 14. Each bottle should now have a scale on its side. Label the 12, 11, and 10 cm marks.

3. Set the small plastic bottle on top of the coffee can. The hole should face outward, and the bottle should sit on the edge of the can.

4. Use your plastic container and funnel to add water to the plastic bottle. Make sure one member of your group plugs the hole in the bottle so that water does not escape. Fill the bottle to the 12 cm mark. If you fill the bottle too full, lift your finger off the hole to allow some water to escape.

5. Place the meterstick at the top of the coffee can. The "0" end of the meterstick should be next to the bottle, with higher numbers moving outward. One member of the group will need to hold the meterstick in place because it will stick out away from the coffee can.

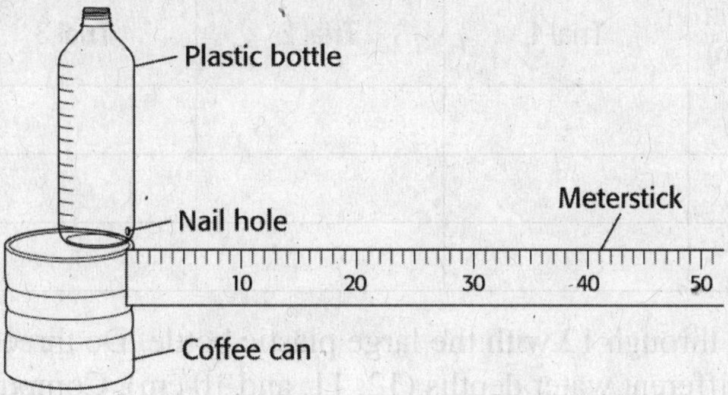

FORM A PREDICTION

6. Make a prediction about what will happen when your finger is lifted off the hole.

____

TEST THE PREDICTION

7. Release your finger from the hole. (If you are doing this lab indoors, catch as much water that pours from the bottle as possible in the plastic container.) When you do, one member of the group reads the exact mark where the water hits the meterstick. Record the distance in the table on the next page.

8. Repeat this trial two more times. Each time, measure how far water will squirt from the small bottle when it is filled to a depth of 12 cm.

9. Compute the average distance by adding the three distances and dividing by three. Record this number in the last column of the table.

10. Repeat the experiment again, this time with the water depth at 11 cm. Do three trials, recording the distance for each trial. Then, compute the average distance the water travels when it is at the 11 cm mark.

Field Lab continued

11 Repeat one more time, this time with the water depth at 10 cm. Do three trials, then compute the average.

DISTANCE WATER SQUIRTS WITH SMALL BOTTLE

Depth of water in small bottle (cm)	Trial 1	Trial 2	Trial 3	Average
12				
11				
10				

12 Repeat Steps 3 through 12 with the large plastic bottle. Do three trials for each of three different water depths (12, 11, and 10 cm). Compute the average for each depth of water.

DISTANCE WATER SQUIRTS WITH LARGE BOTTLE

Depth of water in large bottle (cm)	Trial 1	Trial 2	Trial 3	Average
12				
11				
10				

ANALYZE THE RESULTS

13 **Making Graphs** Display the data in graph form below. On the x-axis, put labels for the depths of 12, 11, and 10 cm. On the y-axis, put labels for the distances the water squirted. Plot the distances for the small bottle with one colored pencil. Plot the distances for the large bottle using a different color.

14 **Explaining Concepts** Was the water depth greater when the bottle was more full or more empty?

____

Field Lab continued

15 **Comparing Results** Did the water squirt farther when the bottle was more full or more empty?

____

16 **Examining Tables** Look at your data tables and graphs. When the height of the water was the same, did the water squirt farther when you used the small bottle or big bottle?

____

DRAW CONCLUSIONS

17 **Making Hypotheses** Form a hypothesis with your group to explain your results.

____

____

18 **Identifying Constraints** What possible limitations or errors did you experience or could you have experienced in this lab?

____

____

19 **Applying Conclusions** Dams are large walls that are built up to hold back lakes or rivers. Why do you think they are thicker and stronger at the bottom than at the top?

____

____

20 **Explaining Concepts** Sometimes your ears can hurt if you dive to the bottom of a swimming pool. Explain why this part of your body can hurt in deep water. Think about what you know about water pressure and depth.

____

____

Connect TO THE ESSENTIAL QUESTION

21 **Applying Concepts** How did the pressure differ in each bottle, and how did this pressure difference affect the motion of the fluids?

____

FIELD LAB GUIDED Inquiry

Pressure in Fluids

In this lab, you will investigate the relationship between the depth of water and the pressure of water. You will poke a hole in plastic bottles, fill them with water, and measure how far water squirts out of the hole. You will create tables to display the data you collect. You'll then work with your group to form a hypothesis about water pressure and water depth.

OBJECTIVE

- Investigate the relationship between water pressure and water depth.

MATERIALS

For each group

- bottle, large
- bottle, small
- can, coffee
- container, plastic
- funnel
- marker, permanent
- meterstick
- nail
- pencil, colored (2)
- ruler, metric
- water

For each student

- lab apron
- safety goggles

PROCEDURE

BUILD A MODEL

1. Use a nail to carefully poke a hole in the side of each bottle. The hole should be close to the bottom of the bottle, as shown in the image below.

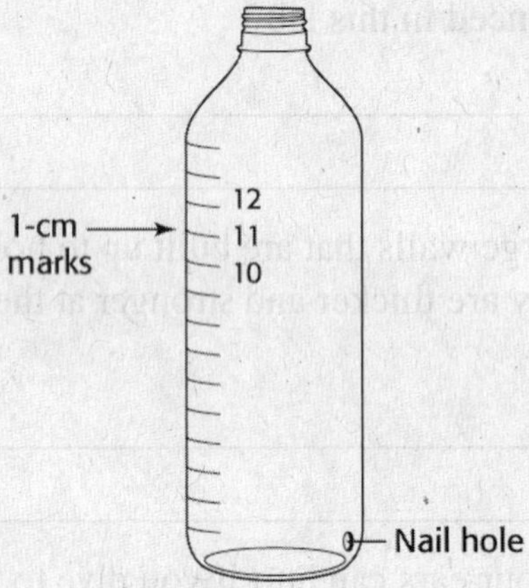

2. Use your ruler and your permanent marker to mark off 1 centimenter (cm) increments on each bottle. Lower numbers should be at the bottom; start with 0 and go to 14. Each bottle should now have a scale on its side. Label the 12, 11, and 10 cm marks.

3. Set the small plastic bottle on top of the coffee can. The hole should face outward, and the bottle should sit on the edge of the can.

4. Use your plastic container and funnel to add water to the plastic bottle. Make sure one member of your group plugs the hole in the bottle so that water does not escape. Fill the bottle to the 12 cm mark. If you fill the bottle too full, lift your finger off the hole to allow some water to escape.

Field Lab continued

5. Place the meterstick at the top of the coffee can. The "0" end of the meterstick should be next to the bottle, with higher numbers moving outward. One member of the group will need to hold the meterstick in place because it will stick out away from the coffee can.

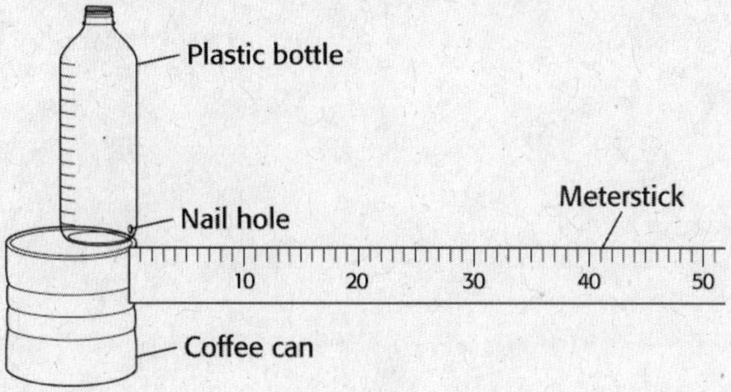

FORM A PREDICTION

6. Make a prediction about what will happen when your finger is lifted off the hole. How far will water squirt?

____

TEST THE PREDICTION

7. Release your finger from the hole. (If you are doing this lab indoors, catch as much water as possible that pours from the bottle in the plastic container.) When you do, one member of the group reads the exact mark where the water hits the meterstick. Record the distance.

8. Repeat this trial two more times. Each time, measure how far water will squirt from the small bottle when it is filled to a depth of 12 cm.

9. Compute the average distance by adding the three distances and dividing by three. Record your measurements.

10. Repeat the experiment again, this time with the water depth at 11 cm. Do three trials, recording the distance for each trial. Then, compute the average distance the water travels when it is at the 11 cm mark.

11. Repeat one more time, this time with the water depth at 10 cm. Do three trials, then compute the average.

12 Create a table to display your data for all three trials. Your table should have data for each depth (12, 11, and 10 cm), measurements from three different trials, and averages.

13 Repeat Steps 3 through 12 with the large plastic bottle. Do three trials for each of three different water depths (12, 11, and 10 cm). Compute the average for each depth of water. Create another table to display this data.

ANALYZE THE RESULTS

14 **Making Graphs** Display the data differently by creating a graph. Work with your group to determine the appropriate labels for the x- and y-axis. Plot the distances for the small bottle with one color pencil. Plot the distances for the large bottle with a different color.

Field Lab continued

15 **Explaining Concepts** Was the water depth greater when the bottle was more full or more empty?

---

16 **Comparing Results** Did the water squirt farther when the bottle was more full or more empty?

---

17 **Examining Tables** Look at your data tables and graphs. When the height of the water was the same, did the water squirt farther when you used the small bottle or big bottle?

DRAW CONCLUSIONS

18 **Making Hypotheses** Form a hypothesis with your group to explain your results.

---

19 **Identifying Constraints** What possible limitations or errors did you experience or could you have experienced in this lab?

---

20 **Applying Conclusions** Dams are large walls that are built up to hold back lakes or rivers. Why do you think they are thicker and stronger at the bottom than at the top?

---

21 **Explaining Concepts** Sometimes your ears can hurt if you dive to the bottom of a swimming pool. Explain why this part of your body can hurt in deep water. Think about what you know about water pressure and depth.

Connect TO THE ESSENTIAL QUESTION

22 **Applying Concepts** How did the pressure differ in each bottle, and how did this pressure difference affect the motion of the fluids?

QUICK LAB DIRECTED *Inquiry*

Investigating Work GENERAL

Student pairs
15 minutes

MATERIALS

For each pair
- meterstick
- notebook, spiral
- spring scale

LAB RATINGS LESS ⟷ MORE

Teacher Prep —
Student Setup —
Cleanup —

My Notes

TEACHER NOTES

In this activity, students will investigate how much work is done when they lift a notebook from the floor to their shoulders. They will then use this information to estimate how much work they do every day when they pick up all their notebooks to take them to school.

Tip Have students compare their results with partners to observe how height affects the amount of work done.

Student Tip Not all forces do work. If the distance an object moves equals zero, then no work is done. For example, the force you exert pushing on a wall equals zero work because the wall does not move.

Skills Focus Making Observations, Analyzing Data

MODIFICATION FOR INDEPENDENT *Inquiry*

Allow students to develop their own procedures for using spring scales to investigate work. Students may determine what objects to move, how to record data, and how to calculate results. Students may also observe how the amount of work done changes depending on the distance the object moves. Once students have completed their investigations, invite them to share their results with the class.

Quick Lab continued

Answer Key

3. Answers will vary depending on the size of the notebook and the height of the student. A typical 3 subject notebook exerts a force of about 4 N.
Sample answer: If the notebook were raised to a height of 1 m, the work done would be 4 N × 1 m or 4 joules.
Teacher Prompt What is the equation you use to calculate work? What are the values you need for the equation?

4. Sample answer: The work would be greater because the notebook would move a longer distance.
Teacher Prompt If you were taller, would the notebook move a shorter distance or a longer distance? If the distance is longer, does work increase or decrease?

5. Sample answer: No work is done if you stop moving the book. When the book is still, the distance moved is zero. Any force multiplied by zero results in work equal to zero.
Teacher Prompt What is the distance that the book moves in this situation? Consider the equation for work. Is any work done if the value for distance is zero?

Name ______________________ Class ______________ Date ________________

QUICK LAB DIRECTED Inquiry

Investigating Work

In this lab, you will investigate how much work is done when you lift a notebook from the floor to your shoulders. Work is force multiplied by distance, and is measured in newton-meters (N·m) or joules (J). One N·m equals one joule.

OBJECTIVES

- Calculate work given force and distance.
- Decide whether work is done based on the direction of motion of an object.

MATERIALS

For each pair

- meterstick
- notebook, spiral
- spring scale

PROCEDURE

1. Have a partner help you measure the distance from the ground to the top of your shoulder. Round to the nearest tenth of a meter and record the distance in the table in Step 3.
2. Attach the notebook to the spring scale. Then slowly lift the notebook to your shoulders and observe the reading on the spring scale. Record the force in newtons in the table in Step 3.
3. Calculate the work you did when lifting one notebook. Use this information to estimate how much work you do every day when you pick up all your notebooks to take them to school. Do the calculations on the back of this sheet.

Distance from floor to shoulder (m)	Force needed to lift notebook (N)	Work done (J)	Estimated work to lift all notebooks (J)

Quick Lab continued

4 How would the amount of work you do change if you were taller? Why?

____

____

____

____

5 How much work are you doing if you stop moving the notebook to talk to a friend? Explain.

____

____

____

____

QUICK LAB DIRECTED Inquiry

Calculating Power BASIC

Student pairs

40 minutes

LAB RATINGS

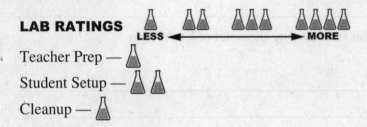

LESS ⟵ ⟶ MORE

Teacher Prep — 1

Student Setup — 2

Cleanup — 1

MATERIALS

For each pair
- books
- cardboard box
- chair
- meterstick
- roller skate
- spring scale
- stopwatch
- string
- weighted measures
- wooden plank, 1 meter long

For each student
- safety goggles

TEACHER NOTES

In this activity, students will calculate power by pushing boxes of weighted measures up ramps and determining which took more power. If time permits, extend the activity by having students figure out the mechanical advantage of using a roller skate to move the box up the hill. If a wooden plank is unavailable, heavy cardboard can be used.

Tip If you are unable to find roller skates, anything with wheels will work to successfully complete this activity.

Student Tip Time is needed to calculate power; speed is not important.

Skills Focus Organizing Data, Analyzing Data, Making Predictions

MODIFICATION FOR INDEPENDENT Inquiry

Have each pair of students think of a scenario in which they can calculate power and design a way to carry out their plan. Allow pairs to carry out any reasonable plans.

My Notes

Quick Lab continued

Answer Key

3. Accept all reasonable answers.
4. Accept all reasonable answers.
5. Power = work ÷ time.
6. Sample answer: I can use the data in the chart to calculate work (work = force × distance). I know the force and the distance, so I can calculate work and divide by time.
7. Accept all reasonable answers.
8. Accept all reasonable answers.
9. Students will notice that the heavier an object, the more work was needed to move it. They will also notice that the same weight always took more power to move up a higher hill.
10. Sample answer: Using the roller skate might decrease the force needed to move the box. Therefore, it would require less power to complete the task. I can test my hypothesis by using a roller skate to move the box of weight, record the force, and recalculate the power with the new data.

Name ______________________ Class ________________ Date ____________________

QUICK LAB DIRECTED Inquiry

Calculating Power

In this lab, you will use the formula for power to calculate the amount of power needed to move different weights up a hill. You will test several variables and use your data to discover any patterns.

OBJECTIVE

- Calculate the amount of power needed to complete a job.

MATERIALS

For each pair
- books
- cardboard box
- chair
- meterstick
- roller skate
- spring scale
- stopwatch
- string
- weighted measures
- wooden plank

For each student
- safety goggles

PROCEDURE

1. Using **books, a chair,** and a **wooden plank**, build a ramp that is 0.5 meters high. This represents a large hill.
2. Fill a **cardboard box** with **weighted measures** equaling 2 newtons. Attach a **spring scale** to the box and place the box at the bottom of the hill.
3. Drag the box up the hill. Use the **stopwatch** to determine how long it took. Record the force and amount of time it took to complete the task. Enter the data into the chart.

Trial 1	Weight	Force	Time	Power
1	2 N			
2	4 N			
3	6 N			
4	8 N			

4. Repeat steps 2 and 3 using weights of 4 newtons, 6 newtons, and 8 newtons.
5. What is the formula for power?

____

6. How can you use the data in the chart and what you know about the setup to calculate power?

____

____

Quick Lab continued

7. Calculate the power used in each trial. Record the information in the chart.

8. Raise the incline of the hill to 1 meter. Repeat Steps 2, 3, 4, and 6. Record your data.

Trail 1	Weight	Force	Time	Power
1	2 N			
2	4 N			
3	6 N			
4	8 N			

Show your work.

____

____

____

9. Do you notice any patterns in your data?

____

____

____

____

10. Do you think the results would change if you placed a roller skate underneath the cardboard box? Explain. Test your prediction.

____

____

____

____

____

____

S.T.E.M. LAB DIRECTED *Inquiry* **AND** GUIDED *Inquiry*

Using Water to Do Work GENERAL

Small groups
45 minutes

LAB RATINGS

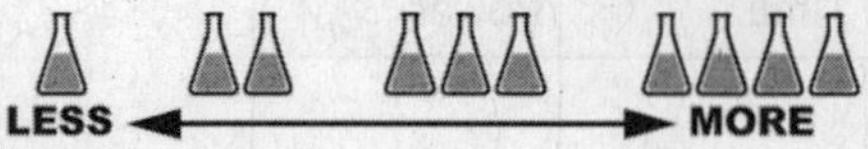

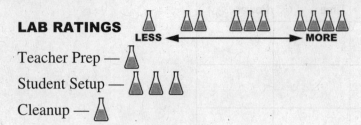

Teacher Prep — 

Student Setup — 

Cleanup — 

SAFETY INFORMATION

Remind students to review all safety cautions and icons before beginning this lab. Allow students to wear lab aprons to keep their clothes dry. Water makes surfaces slippery, so caution students to be careful walking.

TEACHER NOTES

In this activity, students will make simple waterwheels and use them to lift weights. Prepare each 2-liter bottle by drilling a 3/8 hole in the bottom of the bottles. Students will use these holes to slide the dowel through the bottle. You may also want to prefold some index cards so students can see exactly how to create the index-card catchers. You may want to have calculators ready for students who need help with the calculations.

Because students are pouring water onto their wheels, have them perform the experiment over a sink, over a basin, or outside.

Tip This activity may help students better understand the different types of alternative energy sources. As an extension, have students choose a type of alternative energy and present what they find to the class.

Skills Focus Constructing Models, Applying Concepts

MODIFICATION FOR INDEPENDENT *Inquiry*

Ask student groups to think of a way to use water to do work. Have them research the topic and present a plan to build a water-powered machine. Tell them they must calculate the power of their machine. Allow groups to carry out all reasonable and safe plans. Have groups share their work with the class. Display finished machines.

MATERIALS

For each group

- 2-liter bottle drilled
- dowel, ¼ inch diameter
- funnel
- index cards, 8
- marker
- meterstick
- pitcher
- scissors
- stopwatch
- string, 1 meter
- tape
- water
- weight, 50 g

For each student

- lab apron
- safety goggles

My Notes

S.T.E.M. Lab continued

Answer Key for DIRECTED Inquiry

ASK A QUESTION

1. Accept all reasonable answers.

BUILD A MODEL

2. Axle
7. Sample answer: The weight of the water in the catchers causes the bottle to spin, which causes the string to pull up, which lifts the weight.

ANALYZE THE RESULTS

8. 0.98 N
9. Work = force × distance; answers will vary.
10. Power = work ÷ time; answers will vary.

DRAW CONCLUSIONS

11. Sample answer: The water would flow more quickly, which would cause the wheel to turn more quickly.
12. Sample answer: It should increase because more distance means a greater force pushing the wheel.
13. Sample answer: Reduce either the amount of the water or the distance the water is dropped from.
14. Sample answer: It is a renewable resource. It is also a clean resource.

Connect TO THE ESSENTIAL QUESTION

15. Sample answer: Yes, the experiment would work. The wind source would have to be positioned to the side of the wheel, rather than atop it.

S.T.E.M. Lab continued

Answer Key for GUIDED Inquiry

ASK A QUESTION

1. Accept all reasonable answers.

PLAN A MODEL

2. Accept all reasonable answers.
3. Accept all reasonable drawings.
4. Sample answer: I need to use the stopwatch to determine the time it takes to raise the weight and the meterstick to determine the height (or distance) the weight is raised to.

EVALUATE THE PLAN

5. Answers will vary.
6. Answers will vary.
7. Answers will vary.
8. Accept all reasonable drawings.

ANALYZE THE RESULTS

9. 0.98 N
10. Work = force × distance; answers will vary.
11. Power = work ÷ time; answers will vary.

DRAW CONCLUSIONS

12. Sample answer: The water would flow more quickly, which would cause the wheel to turn more quickly.
13. Sample answer: It should increase because more distance means a greater force pushing the wheel.
14. Sample answer: Reduce either the amount of the water or the distance the water is dropped from.
15. Sample answer: It is a renewable resource. It is also a clean resource.

Connect TO THE ESSENTIAL QUESTION

16. Sample answer: Yes, the experiment would work. The wind source would have to be positioned to the side of the wheel, rather than atop it.

Name ______________________ Class ______________ Date ______________

S.T.E.M. LAB DIRECTED Inquiry

Using Water to Do Work

A waterwheel uses the energy of water to do work. Waterwheels can be used to generate electricity, making them a great source of renewable energy. In this lab, you will build a waterwheel and measure the amount of work done.

OBJECTIVES

- Construct a simple wheel that uses the power of water to do work.
- Use formulas to calculate work and power.

MATERIALS

For each group

- 2-liter bottle, drilled
- dowel, ¼ inch diameter
- funnel
- index cards, 8
- marker
- meterstick
- pitcher
- scissors
- stopwatch
- string, 1 meter
- tape
- water
- weight, 50 g

For each student

- lab apron
- safety goggles

PROCEDURE

ASK A QUESTION

1. In this lab, you will investigate the following question: How does a waterwheel work? Write any thoughts you have about the question below.

____

____

____

____

BUILD A MODEL

2. Slide the **dowel** through the **bottle**. If the bottle represents the wheel, what does the dowel represent?

____

3. Use the **marker** to draw six to eight lines lengthwise around the bottle. Make sure there is an equal distance between the lines. These lines represent where the water catchers will be placed.

4. Fold up the sides of the **index cards** to create little boxes to catch the water. Attach one index card catcher on each of the lines you drew in Step 2.

5. Tie one end of the **string** to the neck of the bottle. Tie the other end around the **weight**.

6. Have two students hold each end of the dowel. One student should hold the **funnel** above the waterwheel, while another pours **water** into the funnel.

S.T.E.M. Lab continued

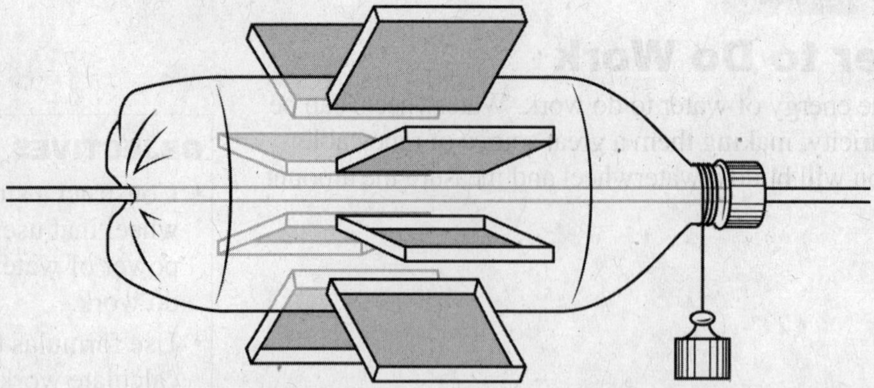

7 Observe what happens. Measure the distance the weight mass is raised. Use the **stopwatch** to record how long it takes. Record your observations below.

ANALYZE THE RESULTS

8 **Applying Concepts** Find the force or weight of the mass by multiplying the mass times gravity. Use 9.8 m/s^2 for gravity and kilograms for mass.

9 **Applying Data** What is the formula for work? Use that formula to calculate the work done by the waterwheel.

10 **Applying Data** How can you find the power of the waterwheel? Calculate the power.

Name ______________________ Class ____________ Date ________________

S.T.E.M. Lab continued

DRAW CONCLUSIONS

11 **Describing Models** What would happen if you poured the water directly on the waterwheel, instead of through the funnel first?

12 **Making Predictions** If you increased the distance between the funnel and the waterwheel, how would the movement of the wheel change? Explain.

13 **Identifying Constraints** How could you slow the movement of the wheel?

14 **Recognizing Costs and Benefits** What are some of the benefits of using the energy of water to do work?

Connect TO THE ESSENTIAL QUESTION

15. **Constructing Models** Would this setup work with wind energy? How would the setup need to be modified?

Name _______________________ Class ______________ Date _______________

S.T.E.M. LAB GUIDED Inquiry

Using Water to Do Work

A waterwheel uses the energy of water to do work. Waterwheels can be used to generate electricity, making them a great source of renewable energy. In this lab, you will build a waterwheel and measure the amount of work done.

OBJECTIVES

- Construct a simple wheel that uses the power of water to do work.
- Use formulas to calculate work and power.

MATERIALS

For each group

- 2-liter bottle, drilled
- dowel, ¼ inch diameter
- funnel
- index cards, 8
- marker
- meterstick
- pitcher
- scissors
- stopwatch
- string, 1 meter
- tape
- water
- weight, 50 g

For each student

- lab apron
- safety goggles

PROCEDURE

ASK A QUESTION

1. In this lab, you will investigate the following question: How does a waterwheel work? Write any thoughts you have about the question below.

____

____

____

____

PLAN A MODEL

2. Look at the materials. How can you use them to build a waterwheel that will lift the weight?

____

____

____

____

____

____

____

____

____

3. Draw a picture of your design.

4. Determine what data you will need to collect to calculate work and power. How do you intend to collect that data?

EVALUATE THE PLAN

5. Show your plan and sketch to your teacher. Once they have been approved, carry out your procedure. Record your observations.

6. How can you improve your design?

7. Carry out the procedure again, this time incorporating the changes from Step 6. Record your observations.

8. Draw a picture of your final design.

ANALYZE THE RESULTS

9. **Applying Concepts** Find the force or weight of the mass by multiplying the mass times gravity. Use 9.8 m/s^2 for gravity and kilograms for mass.

10. **Applying Data** What is the formula for work? Use that formula to calculate the work done by the waterwheel.

11. **Applying Data** How can you find the power of the waterwheel? Calculate the power.

DRAW CONCLUSIONS

12 **Describing Models** What would happen if you poured the water directly on the waterwheel, instead of through the funnel first?

13 **Making Predictions** If you increased the distance between the funnel and the waterwheel, how would the movement of the wheel change? Explain.

14 **Identifying Constraints** How could you slow the movement of the wheel?

15 **Recognizing Costs and Benefits** What are some of the benefits of using the energy of water to do work?

Connect TO THE ESSENTIAL QUESTION

16 **Constructing Models** Would this setup work with wind energy? How would the setup need to be modified?

QUICK LAB INDEPENDENT Inquiry

Investigate Potential Energy ADVANCED

Small groups
30 minutes

LAB RATINGS LESS ← → MORE

Teacher Prep — 1
Student Setup — 2
Cleanup — 1

MATERIALS

For each group
- boards, wood (2)
- books
- carts (2)
- mass, 200-g (1)

For each student
- safety goggles

My Notes

____

____

____

____

____

SAFETY INFORMATION

Remind students to review all safety cautions and icons before beginning this lab.

TEACHER NOTES

In this activity, students will design an investigation to explore how gravitational potential energy relates to the mass of an object and its height of an object above a surface. If student groups struggle when devising their investigations, remind them that potential energy is converted to kinetic energy as an object rolls down a ramp. If an object is held at a certain height above the ground, the amount of potential energy that an object starts with is proportional to the amount of kinetic energy it has after it is released. Have students consider how they could measure the final kinetic energy of an object. To do this, students may need to draw an additional relationship between kinetic energy and another variable. For example, students may note that if two objects have the same mass but different speeds, the faster object has more kinetic energy. One example of an investigation might have students observing how quickly an object rolls after it is released from ramps secured at different angles. Students do not need to perform any calculations for this lab. Instead, they will make qualitative assessments of the effects of height and mass on potential energy.

Student Tip Potential energy is converted to kinetic energy as an object rolls down a ramp. If an object is held at a certain height above a surface, the amount of potential energy that an object starts with is proportional to the amount of kinetic energy it has after it is released. Think about how you can relate the initial height of an object to the final kinetic energy of an object.

Skills Focus Developing Procedures, Analyzing Data

Quick Lab continued

MODIFICATION FOR GUIDED Inquiry

Provide students with a procedure for comparing the kinetic energy of carts at various heights and masses. Have students use the boards and books to make two ramps of different heights and inclines. Students should think of a way to release two carts of equal mass from the ramps at the same time. Students should observe that the cart on the steeper ramp will reach the floor first. Then, have students make two ramps of equal heights and inclines. Students should think of a way to release two carts of different mass from the ramps at the same time. Students should observe that the more massive cart will reach the floor first. After students conduct their investigations, have them share their methods with the class and compare results.

Answer Key

1. Accept all reasonable answers.
Teacher Prompt How is an object's speed related to its kinetic energy? How is kinetic energy related to potential energy?

2. Accept all reasonable answers.

4. Sample answer: The potential energy of the object increased as the height of the object above the floor increased. This is supported by the fact that the object that was released from a greater height reached the end of the ramp before the object that was released from a lower height.

5. Sample answer: The potential energy of the object increased as the mass of the object increased. This is supported by the fact that the more massive object reached the end of the ramp before the less massive object released from the same height.

Name ______________________ Class ______________ Date ________________

QUICK LAB INDEPENDENT *Inquiry*

Investigate Potential Energy

In this activity, you will design an investigation to explore the relationship between the gravitational potential energy of an object, its mass, and its height above a surface. As you work, consider how the initial potential energy of the object relates to its final kinetic energy.

OBJECTIVES

- Explore the relationship between gravitational potential energy, mass, and height.
- Calculate the potential energy of an object.

MATERIALS

For each group
- boards, wood (2)
- books
- carts (2)
- mass, 200-g (1)

For each student
- safety goggles

PROCEDURE

1. Think about how you could explore the relationship between the gravitational potential energy of an object and its height and mass. What independent and dependent variables could you measure?

   ____

2. Review the available materials. Then, write out a procedure that uses these materials to test the relationship between height, mass, and gravitational potential energy.

   ____

   ____

   ____

   ____

   ____

   ____

3. Ask your teacher for approval of your plan. Then carry out your investigation. Record your observations on a separate sheet of paper.

4. Did you observe a relationship between potential energy and height? If so, what was this relationship? Support your response with data from this investigation.

   ____

   ____

   ____

Quick Lab continued

5 Did you observe a relationship between potential energy and mass? If so, what was this relationship? Support your response with data from this investigation.

____

____

____

QUICK LAB DIRECTED *Inquiry*

Identify Potential and Kinetic Energy GENERAL

Small groups
20 minutes

MATERIALS

For each group
- ball
- paper
- pencil
- spring toy
- string
- tape, masking
- washer

LAB RATINGS

LESS ← → MORE

Teacher Prep — 1
Student Setup — 2
Cleanup — 2

My Notes

SAFETY INFORMATION

Remind students to review all safety cautions before beginning this lab. Caution students to attach the pendulum bobs and anchors securely so that the pendulum remains intact and does not pose a hazard to other students.

TEACHER NOTES

In this activity, students will identify potential and kinetic energy in various physical scenarios. Students will set up three different scenarios: a ball dropping to the floor, a washer swinging on a string, and a coiled spring stretching and compressing. They will make observations during these scenarios and then describe how kinetic and potential energy change in each situation. If washers are not available to use as pendulum bobs, students can substitute any other small object that can be tied to a string.

Student Tip For the pendulum scenario, treat the lowest point on the washer's path as a point where there is zero potential energy.

Tip This activity will help students understand the relationship between kinetic and potential energy in different situations.

Skills Focus Making Observations

MODIFICATION FOR GUIDED *Inquiry*

Provide students with the materials and challenge them to create three different scenarios that demonstrate potential and kinetic energy transfer.

Quick Lab continued

Answer Key

5. Students should label points on their sketches at which kinetic energy is the greatest: right before the ball hits the floor, at the bottom of the pendulum, and at the spring's greatest speed after it is released. Students should label points on their sketches at which potential energy is the greatest: before the ball is dropped, at the highest point of the pendulum swing, and when the spring is fully compressed.

6. Sample answer: The object has gravitational potential energy during the ball dropping and pendulum scenarios. The object has elastic potential energy during the compressed spring scenario.
Teacher Prompt In which situations does the object move vertically?

7. Sample answer: Some kinetic energy is converted to potential energy. Some potential energy is converted to kinetic energy. The mechanical energy of the system is equal to the gravitational or elastic potential energy plus the kinetic energy.
Teacher Prompt What happens to the kinetic energy in the system when the potential energy decreases? What happens to the potential energy in the system when the kinetic energy decreases?

8. Sample answer: With each energy conversion, some energy is "lost" through friction. Eventually, all of this energy is released to the surroundings and the motion of the objects stops.

Name ______________________ Class ______________ Date ______________

QUICK LAB DIRECTED Inquiry

Identify Potential and Kinetic Energy

In this activity, you will explore potential and kinetic energy in three different physical scenarios. You will observe a ball dropping to the ground, a washer swinging on a string, and a spring stretching and compressing. Remember that potential energy is energy stored in an object while kinetic energy is the energy of motion.

OBJECTIVES

- Identify potential and kinetic energy in a physical scenario.
- Describe how potential and kinetic energy transfer from one to the other.

MATERIALS

For each group

- ball
- paper
- pencil
- spring toy
- string
- tape, masking
- washer

PROCEDURE

1. Hold the ball at rest approximately 1 meter above the ground. Then, release the ball. Draw a sketch of the ball's path after it is released.

2. Tape the pencil securely to a desk so that half of the pencil extends over the edge of the desk. (Be sure that the sharper edge of the pencil is not pointing outward.) Tie a string to the end of the pencil extending over the edge of the desk. Tie a washer to the loose end of the string.

3. Lift the washer so that the pendulum makes a 45° angle with the floor. Then release the washer from rest. Draw a sketch of the washer's path after it is released.

Quick Lab continued

4. Place the spring toy horizontally on a desk. Hold one end of the spring so that it is fixed. Push in the other end of the spring so that it is compressed. Then, release the end of the spring. Draw a sketch of the spring after it is released.

5. Label each of your sketches by indicating the points along the object's path where kinetic energy is greatest and where potential energy is greatest.

6. In which scenario(s) does the object have gravitational potential energy? In which scenario(s) does the object have elastic potential energy?

____

____

7. How do kinetic and potential energy relate to each other in each scenario? How do these relate to the mechanical energy in each system?

____

____

____

____

8. In each scenario, why does the motion of the object eventually stop?

____

____

____

EXPLORATION LAB GUIDED *Inquiry* **AND** INDEPENDENT *Inquiry*

Mechanical Energy GENERAL

Small groups
45 minutes

MATERIALS

For each group
- balance
- ball
- board, wood
- books
- calculator
- cart
- masses
- meterstick
- stopwatch
- tape, masking

My Notes

LAB RATINGS

LESS ← → MORE

Teacher Prep — 2
Student Setup — 3
Cleanup — 2

TEACHER NOTES

In this activity, students will design an investigation using either a rubber ball or cart and a ramp that can be adjusted to various heights. Provide students with a box of various balls, carts, and weights. Balls should be of different sizes and different materials. The carts should be able to have a mass added to them and still roll. Students will also need a piece of wood and a stack of books to construct a ramp.

For the Guided Inquiry, students will be given the problem to investigate. For the Independent Inquiry, students will be given a choice of problems to investigate. Students will need a balance in order to measure the mass of a ball or cart. Students will use the data from the investigation to compute the potential energy, kinetic energy, and mechanical energy of the system. Students will need to convert their measurements of mass to kilograms and the height of their ramp to meters.

If you have the probe-ware, it is possible to complete this lab using this technology. If using motion detectors, you may need to add a backing to the cart to increase its size so that the motion detector will pick up the cart's movement.

Tip This activity will help students compute both potential and kinetic energy from data measurements they have taken.

Student Tip Be sure not to make the ramp very high or long.

Skills Focus Devising Procedures, Taking Measurements

MODIFICATION FOR DIRECTED *Inquiry*

Provide students with a specific procedure for them to follow in order to collect the necessary data.

Exploration Lab continued

Answer Key for GUIDED Inquiry

ASK A QUESTION

2. Sample answer: KE = 1/2 (mass)(velocity)^2. GPE = (mass)(acceleration due to gravity)(height). We need to know the mass of the ball, the ball's starting height on the ramp, the distance the ball travels, and the duration of time that the ball travels.

FORM A HYPOTHESIS

3. Sample answer: The mechanical energy will increase as the height of the ramp increases because the potential energy increases.

DEVELOP A PLAN

4. Answers will vary. Sample answer: We decided to change the mass of the ball. We chose two different-sized balls. We built a 50 cm ramp at a height of 15 cm. We measured a distance 50 cm from the bottom of the ramp and placed a piece of tape there to mark it. We decided that we would time the ball from the top of the ramp until it reached the tape and run three trials for each size ball that we used.

TEST THE HYPOTHESIS

5. Sample answer:

Mass of the ball	Height of the ramp	Distance the ball traveled	Time the ball traveled

ANALYZE THE RESULTS

6. Answers will vary with regard to data. The potential energy of the ball increases as the height of the ramp increases. The kinetic energy of the ball increases as the height of the ramp increases.

7. Answers will vary with regard to data. The mechanical energy should be the same whether the ball is at the top of the ramp or at the bottom of the ramp.

8. Answers will vary with regard to data. The mechanical energy of the ball should increase as the ramp height increases due to the increase in potential energy.

DRAW CONCLUSIONS

9. Sample answer: The mechanical energy should increase because the potential energy of the ball increases at the start when the kinetic energy is zero. Since the mechanical energy is the sum of potential energy and kinetic energy, the mechanical energy should increase.

10. Accept all reasonable answers.

Exploration Lab continued

Connect TO THE ESSENTIAL QUESTION

11. Accept all reasonable answers.

Answer Key for INDEPENDENT Inquiry

ASK A QUESTION

2. Sample answer. KE = 1/2 (mass)(velocity)^2. GPE = (mass)(acceleration due to gravity)(height). We need to know the mass of the ball, the ball's starting height on the ramp, the distance the ball travels, and the duration of time that the ball travels.

FORM A HYPOTHESIS

3. Sample answer: The mechanical energy will increase as the height of the ramp increases because its potential energy will increase.

4. Sample answer: The mechanical energy will increase as the mass of the car increases because its potential energy will increase.

DEVELOP A PLAN

5. Sample answer: We decided to change the mass of the cart. First we tried the cart by itself, and then we tried the cart plus a small mass. We built a 50 cm ramp at a height of 15 cm. We measured a distance 50 cm from the bottom of the ramp and placed a piece of tape there to mark it. We decided that we would time the carts from the top of the ramp until they reached the tape and run three trials for each cart that we used.

TEST THE HYPOTHESIS

6. Sample answer:

Mass of the object	Height of the ramp	Distance the cart traveled	Time the cart traveled

ANALYZE THE RESULTS

7. Answers will vary with regard to data. The potential energy of the ball increases as the height of the ramp increases. The kinetic energy of the ball increases as the height of the ramp increases.

8. Answers will vary with regard to data. The mechanical energy should be the same whether the ball is at the top of the ramp or at the bottom of the ramp.

9. Answers will vary with regard to data. The mechanical energy of the ball should increase as the ramp height increases due to the increase in potential energy.

Exploration Lab continued

DRAW CONCLUSIONS

10. Sample answer: The mechanical energy should increase because increasing the ramp height and/or increasing the object's mass will increase the potential energy of the object. Since the mechanical energy is the sum of potential energy and kinetic energy, the mechanical energy should increase if the starting potential energy increases.

11. Accept all reasonable answers.

Connect TO THE ESSENTIAL QUESTION

12. Accept all reasonable answers.

EXPLORATION LAB GUIDED Inquiry

Mechanical Energy

In this lab, you will build a ramp and roll a ball down it. The ramp should be adjustable in height. You will design a method for measuring the distance and time the ball travels in order to compute the speed. You will need to receive approval for your design from your teacher before collecting data. From the data collected in the investigation, you will compute the mechanical energy of the ball.

OBJECTIVE

- Compute mechanical energy.

MATERIALS

For each group
- balance
- ball
- board, wood
- books
- calculator
- cart
- masses
- meterstick
- stopwatch
- tape, masking

PROCEDURE

ASK A QUESTION

1. In this lab, you will investigate the following question: What factors affect mechanical energy?

2. The equation for mechanical energy is as follows:
mechanical energy = potential energy + kinetic energy
What data do you need to determine the potential energy of an object? The kinetic energy?

____

____

____

____

FORM A HYPOTHESIS

3. What do you think will happen to the mechanical energy of the ball if you change the height of the ramp?

____

____

DEVELOP A PLAN

4. Develop a plan for testing your hypothesis. Record your plan on a separate piece of paper. Make sure to describe how you will collect and organize your data. In describing how you will collect your distance data, be specific in how you plan to make your measurements. Once you have developed a plan, ask for your teacher's approval before continuing.

Exploration Lab continued

TEST THE HYPOTHESIS

5. Create a table below to record your data. Your table needs to include a column for the mass of the ball, a column for the height of the ramp, a column for the distance the ball travels, and a column for the duration of time that the ball travels. In addition, include a column for each of the computed values: potential energy, kinetic energy, and mechanical energy.

ANALYZE THE RESULTS

6. **Analyzing Data** At the top of the ramp, how much potential energy did the ball have? How much kinetic energy did it have? Using the data from the table, write a statement that describes the relationship between the height of the ramp with each of the following: potential energy and kinetic energy.

____

____

____

7. **Analyzing Data** Compare the ball's mechanical energy at the top of the ramp with its mechanical energy at the bottom of the ramp for each trial. Are the values the same? Why or why not?

____

____

____

8. **Interpreting Data** Was there a difference in any of the computed values for mechanical energy among the trials? Did the mechanical energy increase, decrease, or stay the same? Explain the reason for these results in a sentence or two.

____

____

____

Exploration Lab continued

DRAW CONCLUSIONS

9 **Making Predictions** What would happen if you both increased the height of the ramp and increased the mass of the ball? Explain your answer based on the data you collected in your investigation.

10 **Evaluating Hypotheses** Review your hypothesis from Step 3. Do your data support your hypothesis? If not, revise your hypothesis below.

Connect TO THE ESSENTIAL QUESTION

11 **Analyzing Data** Explain how to calculate the kinetic, potential, and mechanical energy of an object given its mass, speed, and height.

EXPLORATION LAB INDEPENDENT Inquiry

Mechanical Energy

In this lab, you will need to choose between two scientific investigations. The first investigation will determine how the height of a ramp affects the mechanical energy of a ball. The second investigation determines how the mass of a cart affects its mechanical energy. You will need to design a method for measuring the distance and time the ball or cart travels in order to compute its speed. Remember to receive approval for your design from your teacher before performing the experiment. From the data collected in the investigation, you will compute mechanical energy.

OBJECTIVE

- Compute mechanical energy.

MATERIALS

For each group

- balance
- ball
- board, wood
- books
- calculator
- cart
- masses
- meterstick
- stopwatch
- tape, masking

PROCEDURE

ASK A QUESTION

1. In this lab, you will investigate the following question: What factors affect mechanical energy?

2. The equation for mechanical energy is as follows:
mechanical energy = potential energy + kinetic energy
What data do you need to determine the potential energy of an object? The kinetic energy?

____

____

____

____

FORM A HYPOTHESIS

3. What do you think will happen to the mechanical energy of a ball if you change the height of the ramp it rolls down? Why? State your hypothesis below.

____

____

4. What do you think will happen to the mechanical energy of a cart rolling down a ramp if you change its mass? Why? State your hypothesis below.

____

____

Exploration Lab continued

DEVELOP A PLAN

5. Choose one hypothesis (from Steps 3 and 4) that you and your group want to investigate. Develop a plan for testing your chosen hypothesis. Record your plan on a separate piece of paper. Make sure to describe how you will collect and organize your data, and be specific in how you plan to make your measurements. Once you have developed a plan, ask for your teacher's approval before continuing.

TEST THE HYPOTHESIS

6. Create a table below to record your data. Your table needs to include a column for the mass of the ball or car, a column for the height of the ramp, a column for the distance the ball or car travels, and a column for the duration of time that the ball or car travels. You may wish to include other columns for computed values.

ANALYZE THE RESULTS

7. **Analyzing Data** At the top of the ramp, how much potential energy did the object have? How much kinetic energy did it have? Using the data from the table, write a statement that describes the relationship between the height of the ramp with each of the following: potential energy and kinetic energy.

____

____

____

____

____

8 **Analyzing Data** Compare the object's mechanical energy at the top of the ramp with its mechanical energy at the bottom of the ramp in each trial. Are the values the same? Why or why not?

____

____

____

____

____

9 **Interpreting Data** Was there a difference in any of the computed mechanical energy of the trials? Did the mechanical energy increase, decrease, or stay the same? Explain the reason for these results in a sentence or two.

____

____

____

____

____

DRAW CONCLUSIONS

10 **Making Predictions** What would happen if you increased both the height of the ramp and the mass of the object? Explain your answer based on the data you collected in your investigation.

____

____

____

____

____

11 **Evaluating Hypotheses** Do your data support your hypothesis? If not, revise your hypothesis below.

____

____

____

____

Exploration Lab continued

Connect **TO THE ESSENTIAL QUESTION**

⑫ **Analyzing Data** Explain how to calculate the kinetic, potential, and mechanical energy of an object given its mass, speed, and height.

____

____

____

____

____

QUICK LAB DIRECTED Inquiry

Mechanical Efficiency GENERAL

Small groups
30 minutes

LAB RATINGS

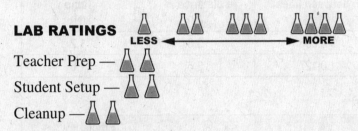

LESS ← → MORE

Teacher Prep — 2
Student Setup — 2
Cleanup — 2

MATERIALS

For each group
- board
- books
- ruler, metric
- spring scale, 5N
- toy cart, approximately 400 g

For each student
- safety goggles

SAFETY INFORMATION

Remind students to review all safety cautions and icons before beginning this lab. Care should be taken by students working with ramps and spring scales.

TEACHER NOTES

In this activity, students will work in groups to build two simple ramps of different heights and measure their dimensions. Using a spring scale, they will measure the input force required to pull a toy cart up the ramps and the output force required to lift the carts straight up. From these, students will calculate the input and output work and the mechanical advantage and efficiency of each ramp.

Students may need assistance in measuring the height of the ramps and recording the values in meters. Centimeters are a more convenient unit, but meters are necessary if the work units are to be expressed in joules.

A significant height difference between the low and high ramps will help ensure that students observe a difference in mechanical advantage between the two ramps.

Tip This classic lab is effective for demonstrating how to quantify the mechanical advantage of a simple machine.

Skills Focus Practicing Lab Techniques, Collecting Data, Analyzing Data

My Notes

MODIFICATION FOR GUIDED Inquiry

To modify for Guided Inquiry, provide students with the same materials, as well as the definitions for a ramp's input and output force, input and output work, and efficiency. Direct the students to develop a plan to use the materials to find a ramp's efficiency. Approve the plan for safety before they begin.

Quick Lab continued

Answer Key

3. Values entered will vary. Sample answers:

Ramp	*L*, distance between lines (m)	*H*, height difference between lines (m)	F_{out}, force required to lift the cart vertically distance *H* (N)	F_{in}, force required to pull cart up the ramp (N)
Low	0.300	0.055	3.6	1.2
High	0.300	0.127	3.6	1.6

7. Values entered will vary. Sample answers:

Ramp	$MA = \frac{F_{out}}{F_{in}}$	$Work_{in} = F_{in}L$ (J)	$Work_{out} = F_{out}H$ (J)	Efficiency % = $\left(\frac{Work_{out}}{Work_{in}}\right) \times 100$
Low	3.0	0.36	0.20	56%
High	2.4	0.48	0.46	96%

8. Sample answer: The low ramp had the greater mechanical advantage.

9. Sample answer: The high ramp had the higher efficiency, probably because it was more similar to the action of the lifting the cart directly. Also, friction was less of a problem because the cart wasn't pressing down on the board as much.

Name ______________________ Class ______________ Date ______________

QUICK LAB DIRECTED Inquiry

Mechanical Efficiency

A ramp is an example of an inclined plane. An inclined plane is one of the simple machines that makes work easier. In this activity, you will compare the mechanical efficiency of two different ramps.

OBJECTIVE

- Build, use, and compare two simple ramps.

MATERIALS

For each group

- board
- books
- ruler, metric
- spring scale, 5N
- toy cart, approximately 400 g

For each student

- safety goggles

PROCEDURE

1. During this activity, you will build two ramps (a low ramp and a high ramp) and use each to move a toy cart to a higher position. Use the books and the board to build each ramp, making sure that the final setups are stable.

2. Begin by building the low ramp as shown in the diagram below. Use the ruler to draw two lines across the upper surface of the board, each about 10 centimeters (cm) from one end. In the table below record the distance in meters along the board between the two lines. This is distance *L* shown in the diagram.

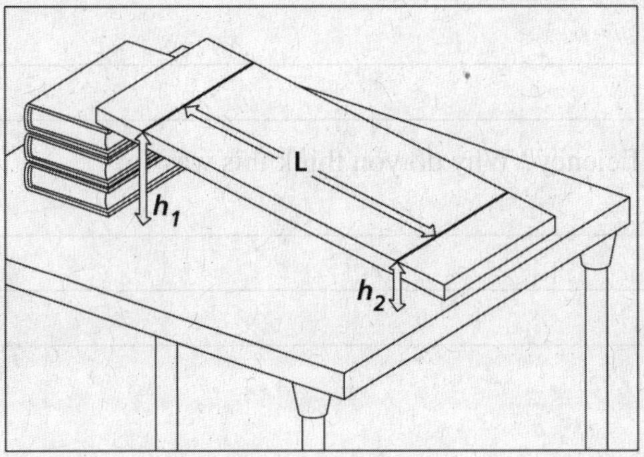

3. Use the ruler to determine the heights h_1 and h_2 as shown in the diagram. Subtract these two values to find the change in height *H* between the lines. Enter the height difference in meters in the table below.

Ramp	*L*, distance between lines (m)	*H*, height difference between lines (m)	F_{out}, force required to lift the cart vertically distance *H* (N)	F_{in}, force required to pull cart up the ramp (N)
Low				
High				

Quick Lab continued

4 Use the spring scale to measure the force F_{out} required to lift the cart a vertical distance H with no help from the ramp. Do this by hanging the cart from the scale. Record the scale reading in newtons in the table above.

5 Use the spring scale to measure the force F_{in} required to tow the cart up the ramp. Try to get a consistent reading of the force required to steadily pull the cart up the ramp. Record the scale reading in the table above.

6 Repeat Steps 2–5 with a ramp that has a steeper incline than your first ramp.

7 Use the formula in the table below to find the experimental mechanical advantage (MA), input work, output work, and mechanical efficiency of each ramp.

Ramp	$MA = \frac{F_{out}}{F_{in}}$	$Work_{in} = F_{in}L$ (joules)	$Work_{out} = F_{out}H$ (joules)	Efficiency % = $\left(\frac{Work_{out}}{Work_{in}}\right) \times 100$
Low				
High				

8 Which ramp had the greater mechanical advantage?

____

____

9 Which ramp had the greater efficiency? Why do you think this was so?

____

____

____

QUICK LAB DIRECTED Inquiry

Investigate Pulleys GENERAL

Small groups
30 minutes

LAB RATINGS LESS ← → MORE

Teacher Prep — 2
Student Setup — 3
Cleanup — 2

MATERIALS

For each group
- marker, permanent
- metersticks (2)
- pulleys (2)
- ring stand
- spring scale, 5 N
- string
- test object, approximately 400 g

For each student
- safety goggles

SAFETY INFORMATION

Remind students to review all safety cautions and icons before beginning this lab. Caution students to keep a grip on the spring scales when measuring the forces on the string. Tell students to be sure that their ring stand assembly is stable so that the pulley system does not topple when pulling the spring scale to lift the object.

My Notes

TEACHER NOTES

In this activity, students will set up and use a simple pulley system and then a 2-pulley block and tackle pulley system to lift a 400 g test object. (Examples could include a bag of beans or coins. A plastic bag of 150 pennies is approximately equal to 400 grams). For each system, they will compare the force required to lift the test object using the pulley system with that needed to lift it directly and calculate the mechanical advantage. Students should draw conclusions comparing the two types of pulleys.

There is so little friction in the lab pulley system that an attempt to calculate mechanical efficiency using spring scales and rulers gets lost in measurement error. However, this activity works well for showing two different ways of calculating mechanical advantage: with distances and with forces.

There should be at least three people per student group.

Skills Focus Practicing Lab Techniques, Comparing Data, Drawing Conclusions

MODIFICATION FOR GUIDED Inquiry

To modify for guided inquiry, provide students with the same equipment and the force and distance definitions for mechanical advantage, as well as diagrams for suggested pulley systems. Have students decide how to use the materials to determine and compare the mechanical advantages of two systems.

Quick Lab continued

Answer Key

6. Accept all reasonable answers.

	F_{in}, force required to lift the test object (N)	D_{in}, distance the string was pulled by the spring scale (m)	Mechanical advantage $= \frac{F_{out}}{F_{in}}$	Mechanical advantage $= \frac{D_{in}}{D_{out}}$
Simple pulley system	4.0	0.11	1.0	1.1
Block and tackle system	2.2	0.22	1.8	2.2

8. Accept all reasonable answers.

9. Accept all reasonable answers. Students should find a mechanical advantage of approximately 1 for the simple pulley system and 2 for the block and tackle system.

10. Sample answer: The block and tackle has the greater mechanical advantage with an MA of 2.

11. Sample answer: The block and tackle would work better for a heavy load because only half as much force would be required to lift it as with the simple pulley.

QUICK LAB DIRECTED Inquiry

Investigate Pulleys

People often use simple machines to lift heavy loads. One such machine is the pulley. In this activity, you will construct two different pulley systems and compare them.

OBJECTIVES

- Construct two pulley systems
- Calculate and compare the mechanical advantages of the two systems.

MATERIALS

For each group

- marker, permanent
- metersticks (2)
- pulleys (2)
- ring stand
- spring scale, 5 N
- string
- test object, approximately 400 g

For each student

- safety goggles

PROCEDURE

1. Using the ring stand as a support, prepare the simple pulley system as shown in the diagram below. Make sure the ring is positioned over the base to reduce the chance that the stand will tip over. Tie a loop at the end of the string for the spring scale hook.

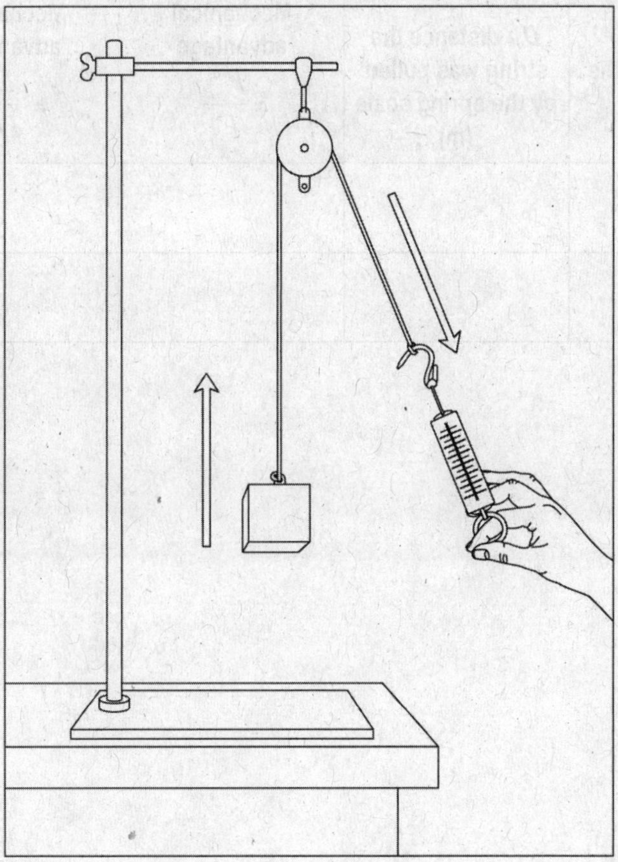

2. Use the spring scale to measure the weight of the test object. Record the value in newtons.

   F_{out} = weight of the test object, N: ______________________

Quick Lab continued

3. Prepare the setup so that you can measure how far the string is pulled. Attach the test object to one end of the string and pass the string over the pulley. Hold the string at the angle you are going to pull it. Then, make a mark on the string where the string first touches the pulley wheel.

4. Work with your group to divide the tasks. One person will use one meterstick to monitor the rise of the load, one person will control and read the spring scale, and one person will use the other meterstick to measure the string length used.

5. Align the mark on the string as you had it in Step 3. Attach the spring scale to the loop in the string, and pull down on the scale to lift the weight. Lift the weight a distance of 10 cm (D_{out} = 0.10 m).

6. In the table below, record the force reading on the spring scale and the distance the string was pulled away from the pulley.

	F_{in}, force required to lift the test object (N)	D_{in}, distance the string was pulled by the spring scale (m)	Mechanical advantage $= \frac{F_{out}}{F_{in}}$	Mechanical advantage $= \frac{D_{in}}{D_{out}}$
Simple pulley system				
Block and tackle system				

Quick Lab continued

7. Next, use both pulleys to prepare the pulley system shown in the diagram below. This arrangement is called a *block and tackle*.

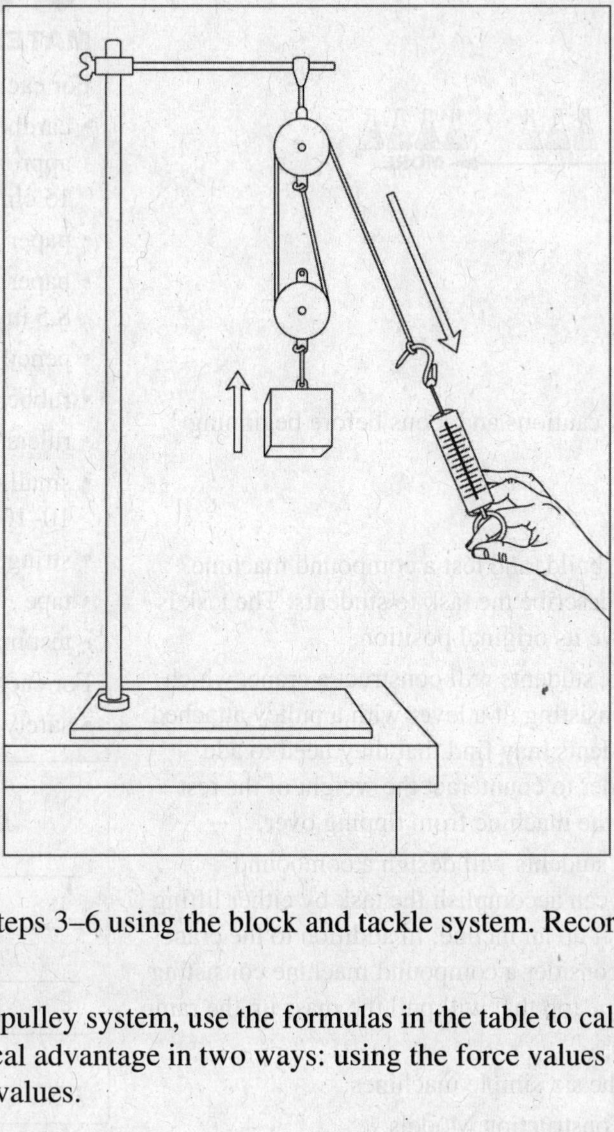

8. Repeat Steps 3–6 using the block and tackle system. Record your data in the table.

9. For each pulley system, use the formulas in the table to calculate the mechanical advantage in two ways: using the force values and using the distance values.

10. Compare the two pulley systems. Which has the greater mechanical advantage?

____

11. Which pulley system would be most useful if the load was very heavy? Explain.

____

____

____

____

S.T.E.M. LAB DIRECTED Inquiry **AND** GUIDED Inquiry

Compound Machines GENERAL

Small groups

90 minutes

MATERIALS

For each group
- cardboard box, approximately 15 cm wide
- paper clip
- paper, 8.5 in. × 11 in.
- pencil
- rubber bands (2)
- rulers, metric (3)
- small masses, 10–100 g
- string, 20 cm long
- tape
- test mass, 100 g

For each student
- safety goggles

My Notes

LAB RATINGS

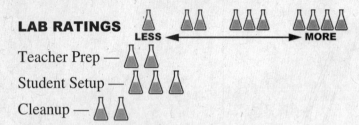

LESS ◄──► MORE

Teacher Prep — 2

Student Setup — 3

Cleanup — 2

SAFETY INFORMATION

Remind students to review all safety cautions and icons before beginning this lab.

TEACHER NOTES

In this activity, students will design, build, and test a compound machine. You will supply the basic parts and describe the task to students. The task is to raise a mass vertically 15 cm above its original position.

In the directed version of this lab, students will construct a crane, which is a common compound machine consisting of a lever with a pulley attached to one end. In this investigation, students may find that they need to add masses to the base of the lever in order to counteract the weight of the test mass being lifted. This will prevent the machine from tipping over.

In the guided version of this lab, students will design a compound machine. Remind students that they can accomplish the task by either lifting an object straight up or by dragging it up an incline. In addition to the crane design, these students may want to consider a compound machine consisting of a ramp with a pulley attached at the top that will pull the mass up the ramp to the indicated height.

Tip If possible, display images of the six simple machines.

Skills Focus Applying Concepts, Construction Models, Making Observations

MODIFICATION FOR INDEPENDENT Inquiry

Show students images of the six simple machines, and explain that compound machines are a combination of at least two simple machines. Explain the task challenge to students, and have them brainstorm and sketch a design for the compound machine. Once students have a design, they should make a list of all materials that could be used to construct and test the machine. Then, students should develop a set of procedures that they could follow in order to determine whether their machines satisfy the task. As students carry out the investigation, encourage them to examine their designs and modify the machines as necessary. Remind students to record all measurements.

S.T.E.M. Lab continued

Answer Key for DIRECTED Inquiry

ASK A QUESTION

2. Sample answer: A crane is a combination of a pulley and a lever.

BUILD A MODEL

14. Answers will vary.

15. Answers will vary.
Teacher Prompt If the cardboard box begins to tip over when too much mass is added to the hook, think about what you could do to counteract the weight on the hook.

ANALYZE THE RESULTS

16. Answers will vary.

17. Sample answer: The two rulers and the cardboard box formed the lever, and the cylinder, string, and pencil formed the pulley system.

DRAW CONCLUSIONS

18. Sample answer: A compound machine is better than a simple machine because it can accomplish more tasks than a simple machine. The lever on the crane was able to anchor the crane to keep it from tipping over, and the pulley was able to lift the mass off the ground.

19. Sample answer: Real-world cranes probably have a lot of mass at the base of the crane to counteract the weight of the objects being lifted.

Connect TO THE ESSENTIAL QUESTION

20. Sample answer: I applied a rotational force to the end of the pencil. The machine redirected my force so that an upward linear force was applied to the test mass.

S.T.E.M. Lab continued

Answer Key for GUIDED Inquiry

ASK A QUESTION

2. Sample answer: Cranes and wheelbarrows are examples of compound machines that can lift objects. A crane is a compound machine consisting of a pulley and a lever. A wheelbarrow is a compound machine consisting of a lever and wheel and axle.

FORM A HYPOTHESIS

5. Answers will vary.

6. Answers will vary.

TEST THE HYPOTHESIS

9. Answers will vary.

ANALYZE THE RESULTS

10. Answers will vary.

11. Answers will vary.

DRAW CONCLUSIONS

12. Sample answer: A compound machine is better than a simple machine because it can accomplish more tasks than a simple machine. The lever on the crane was able to anchor the crane to keep it from tipping over, and the pulley was able to lift the mass off the ground.

13. Sample answer: Real-world cranes probably have a lot of mass at the base of the crane to counteract the weight of the objects being lifted.

Connect TO THE ESSENTIAL QUESTION

14. Sample answer: I applied a rotational force to the end of the pencil. The machine redirected my force so that an upward linear force was applied to the test mass.

Name ______________________ Class ______________ Date ______________

S.T.E.M. LAB DIRECTED *Inquiry*

Compound Machines

In this lab, you will design a compound machine to perform a simple task. A compound machine is a machine made up of two or more simple machines. Your compound machine must be able to move a 100 g mass to a position 15 cm higher than its original position. Your group will design, build, and use a compound machine to complete the task.

OBJECTIVE

- Describe how compound machines apply forces to objects.

MATERIALS

For each group

- cardboard box, approximately 15 cm wide
- paper clip
- paper, 8.5 in. × 11 in.
- pencil
- rubber bands (2)
- rulers, metric (3)
- small masses, 10–100 g
- string, 20 cm long
- tape
- test mass, 100 g

For each student

- safety goggles

PROCEDURE

ASK A QUESTION

1. In this lab, you will investigate the following question: How can two or more simple machines be combined in order to lift an object?

2. Think about a crane. What two simple machines are combined to create a crane?

BUILD A MODEL

3. Stand a **ruler** in one corner of the **cardboard box** so that it is flat against the long side of the box. Then, lean the ruler slightly over the short side of the box. This will be the height of your crane. Use a second ruler to measure the height of the leaning ruler above the desk. (It should be greater than 15 cm.)

4. Use **tape** to secure the ruler to the inside of the box.

5. Repeat this process for a second ruler. Place the second ruler in the corner across from the first ruler so that the two rulers face each other and both lean out over the short edge of the box. Be sure that the second ruler is the same height above the desk as the first ruler. Tape the second ruler to the inside of the box.

6. Roll up a sheet of **paper** to form a tight cylinder. Tape the paper to secure the cylinder.

7. Wrap a large **rubber band** a few times around one end of the cylinder. Then, twist the rubber band once and wrap the rest of the band around the top of one ruler. This should secure one end of the cylinder to one ruler.

8. Wrap a second rubber band around the other end of the cylinder, and then secure that end to the second ruler. The cylinder should be securely attached to both rulers. It should be parallel to the desk.

9. Find a **pencil** that is longer than the width of the cardboard box. You are going to push the pencil through one side of the box and then into the other side. Mark off the spots on the box walls where the pencil will push through. (The location is just beyond the bottom edge of the rulers, near the bottom of the box but not touching the bottom of the box.) Push the pencil through the walls so that it is suspended through the width of the box. The eraser should still poke through the outside of the box. Turn the eraser end of the pencil to be sure that the pencil can spin. This will be the crank for your crane.

10. Tape one end of the **string** to the middle of the pencil. Lift the string and place it so that it hangs over the top of the cylinder.

11. Bend a **paper clip** so that it forms a hook. Tie the free end of the string to the paper clip so that the hook hangs over the cylinder.

12. Turn the eraser end of the pencil. The hook and string should lift up away from the desk.

13. Turn the pencil so that the hook hangs just above the desk. Attach a small **test mass** to the hook.

14. Turn the pencil so that the test mass lifts off the table. When it has reached the maximum height of the crane, use the third ruler to measure this height above the desk. Record the height and mass lifted for this trial.

____

15. Gradually add more mass to the crane, and record the maximum height lifted for each mass. Continue to add mass until the crane satisfies the task requirement for mass and height.

____

____

____

____

____

ANALYZE THE RESULTS

16. **Explaining Events** Did your compound machine successfully perform the task? If not, why do you think it was unsuccessful? If your machine was unsuccessful, make modifications to your design and try again.

____

____

____

____

____

____

17. **Describing Observations** Which materials form the lever in this compound machine? What materials form the pulley system?

____

____

____

____

____

____

____

____

18 **Applying Conclusions** What is the advantage of a compound machine over a simple machine? Use evidence from the investigation to support your response.

____

____

____

____

____

____

____

____

____

19 **Applying Concepts** Large real-world cranes lift extremely heavy loads. Based on your observations in this investigation, how are those cranes able to lift heavy loads without tipping over?

____

____

____

____

____

____

____

____

Connect TO THE ESSENTIAL QUESTION

20 **Analyzing Events** What force did you apply to the crane? How did the machine redirect your force so that a mass was lifted off the desk?

____

____

____

____

____

____

Name ______________________ Class ______________ Date ______________

S.T.E.M. LAB GUIDED Inquiry

Compound Machines

In this lab, you will design a compound machine to perform a simple task. A compound machine is a machine made up of two or more simple machines. Your compound machine must be able to move a 100 g mass to a position 15 cm higher than its original position. Your group will design, build, and use a compound machine to complete the task.

OBJECTIVE

- Describe how compound machines apply forces to objects.

MATERIALS

For each group

- cardboard box, approximately 15 cm wide
- paper clip
- paper, 8.5 in. × 11 in.
- pencil
- rubber bands (2)
- rulers, metric (3)
- small masses, 10–100 g
- string, 20 cm long
- tape
- test mass, 100 g

For each student

- safety goggles

PROCEDURE

ASK A QUESTION

1. In this lab, you will investigate the following question: How can two or more simple machines be combined in order to lift an object?

2. Brainstorm two real-world compound machines that are used to lift large objects. Identify whether each is a simple machine or a compound machine. Identify the simple machines that make up the compound machine.

____

____

____

____

____

____

____

MAKE OBSERVATIONS

3. Consider and observe images of each of the six simple machines.

4. Think about how these simple machines could be used to complete the challenge in this activity.

S.T.E.M. Lab continued

FORM A HYPOTHESIS

5 As a group, brainstorm a design for your compound machine. Sketch a diagram of the machine.

6 Form a hypothesis that states exactly what you are going to build, and explain why you have chosen that design.

TEST THE HYPOTHESIS

7 Gather all supplies needed for the construction of your compound machine. No supplies may be used other than those provided unless your teacher grants specific permission.

S.T.E.M. Lab continued

8. Carefully construct your compound machine to match your sketch and hypothesis statement. Modifications to your original plans should be approved by your teacher.

9. Once construction is complete, operate your machine to see if it will lift the 100 g mass 15 cm above the original position. Take any necessary measurements you think are important and record carefully.

____

____

____

____

____

____

____

ANALYZE THE RESULTS

10. **Explaining Events** Did your compound machine successfully perform the task? If not, why do you think it was unsuccessful? If your machine was unsuccessful, make modifications to your design and try again.

____

____

____

____

____

____

11. **Making Predictions** How could you improve the overall efficiency of your design?

____

____

____

____

____

____

S.T.E.M. Lab continued

DRAW CONCLUSIONS

12 **Applying Conclusions** What is the advantage of a compound machine over a simple machine?

____

____

13 **Applying Concepts** Large real-world cranes lift extremely heavy loads. Based on your observations in this investigation, how are those cranes able to lift heavy loads without tipping over?

____

____

Connect TO THE ESSENTIAL QUESTION

14 **Analyzing Events** What force did you apply to the crane? How did the machine redirect your force so that a mass was lifted off the desk?

____

____

____

____

____

____

QUICK LAB DIRECTED Inquiry

Making a Static Detector ADVANCED

Student pairs
30 minutes

LAB RATINGS LESS ⟷ MORE

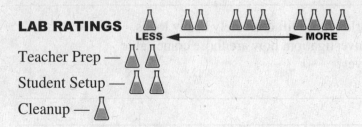

Teacher Prep — 2
Student Setup — 2
Cleanup — 1

MATERIALS

For each pair:
- aluminum foil, balled
- aluminum foil, 1 cm × 4 cm strip
- balloon, inflated
- clay, modeling
- cup, plastic, clear
- paper clip

For each student
- safety goggles

SAFETY INFORMATION

Remind students to review all safety cautions and icons before beginning this lab. Caution students to be careful when straightening the paper clip and inserting it through the paper cup.

My Notes

TEACHER NOTES

In this activity, students will explore the effects of static electricity on a strip of aluminum foil. As a negatively-charged balloon is moved toward the experimental set-up, it repels negative charges from the surface of the aluminum foil ball and attracts positive charges. This causes the charges in the aluminum foil ball and aluminum strip to be temporarily redistributed such that the aluminum strip has a positive charge. This causes the two sides of the strip to repel one another.

Before beginning the activity, cut a small hole at the bottom of a plastic cup so that the paper clip can slide through when it is straightened out. Also, inflate one balloon for each student pair. You may want to inflate a few more in case some break.

Tip If students do not feel comfortable rubbing the balloon on their hair, you may suggest that students rub the balloon on a wool sweater or blanket in the classroom.

Skills Focus Practicing Lab Techniques, Making Observations, Analyzing Results

MODIFICATION FOR GUIDED Inquiry

Provide students with all materials and guide them through the experimental set-up. Do not explain to students that they will rub the balloon on their hair. Challenge students to brainstorm a procedure that will allow them to move the aluminum strip inside the cup without touching the strip or shaking the cup. Prompt students by reminding them that the electric force between charged particles can cause objects to move. After you approve student procedures, allow students to carry out their investigations and have students share their results with the class.

Quick Lab continued

Answer Key

5. Sample answer: The two halves of the strip moved apart from each other.
6. Sample answer: The balloon gains excess negative charges.
7. Sample answer: The negative charges on the surface of the balloon repel the negative charges in the aluminum foil ball.
   Teacher Prompt What charge does the balloon have? What happens when like charges come close to each other?
8. Sample answer: Negative charges from the aluminum ball flow through the metal into the two aluminum strips inside the cup. Because the two halves have the same charge, they repel, or move apart from each other.
   Teacher Prompt If the balloon repels negative charges from the aluminum foil ball, where do those charges go? What is the charge on each half of the aluminum foil strip? How do the charges on the aluminum foil strip interact with each other?
9. Sample answer: If the balloon had a different charge, the aluminum strip halves would still move apart from each other because they would still have like charges.
   Teacher Prompt If the balloon were oppositely charged, what would this do to the charges in the aluminum foil ball? What charge would the aluminum foil strip have?

QUICK LAB DIRECTED Inquiry

Making a Static Detector

In this activity, you will build a device that will allow you to observe the effects of static electricity. As you conduct the investigation, remember that like charges repel, while opposite charges attract.

OBJECTIVES

- Observe ways in which objects can become electrically charged.
- Observe how the electric force can cause objects to move.

MATERIALS

For each pair:

- aluminum foil, balled
- aluminum foil, 1 cm × 4 cm strip
- balloon, inflated
- clay, modeling
- cup, plastic, clear
- paper clip

For each student

- safety goggles

PROCEDURE

1. Bend a paper clip so that it forms a straight line with a hook on the end. Insert the paper clip through the hole in the cup so that the hooked end is inside of the cup and the straight end extends out through the bottom of the cup. Use clay on the outside of the cup to hold the paper clip in place.

2. Stick the ball of foil onto the straight end of the paper clip so that it is attached to the bottom of the cup.

3. Bend the foil strip in half and shape it so it forms an upside-down "V." Then, place the strip on the hooked end of the paper clip so that the two halves of the strip hang down on both sides of the hook.

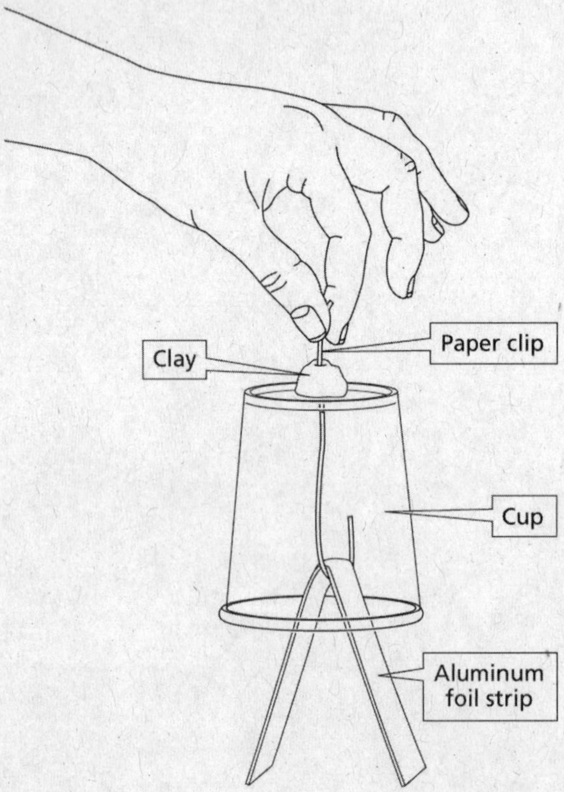

Quick Lab continued

4. Give the balloon a static charge by rubbing it over your hair. Then slowly bring the balloon near the ball of foil on the bottom of the cup. Do not let the balloon touch the foil.

5. Observe the foil strip inside the cup as you move the balloon toward the foil ball. Record your observations below.

____

____

6. What happens to the balloon when you rub it on your hair?

____

____

7. What happens to the charged particles in the aluminum foil ball when you move the balloon toward the ball?

____

____

____

8. Why do the two halves of the aluminum foil strip inside the cup behave this way?

____

____

____

9. Suppose the balloon had the opposite charge of the one you gave it. What would happen to the aluminum foil strip if you brought the balloon near the ball of foil? Explain.

____

____

____

QUICK LAB DIRECTED Inquiry

Investigate Conductors and Insulators GENERAL

Individual student

30 minutes

LAB RATINGS LESS ⟵⟶ MORE

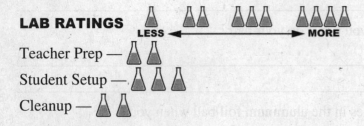

Teacher Prep — 2

Student Setup — 3

Cleanup — 2

MATERIALS

For each student

- aluminum foil
- battery, D-cell
- battery holder
- craft stick
- flashlight bulb with bulb holder
- safety goggles
- spoon, metal
- spoon, plastic
- penny
- wire, insulated copper with alligator clips (3)

SAFETY INFORMATION

Remind students to review all safety cautions and icons before beginning this lab. Caution should always be used when working with batteries and light bulbs. Warn students not to touch any bare copper wire when it is attached to the battery.

TEACHER NOTES

In this activity, students will build a simple circuit and use it to test the conductivity of various materials. To save time, you may wish to set up the circuit for students and have them test the materials. If resources are not available, this activity can be completed in pairs.

Tip You may wish to review the concept of an electric circuit. Use the simple circuit set up for this activity to demonstrate the difference between an open and closed circuit. Once students have demonstrated that they understand the concept of circuits, have them carry out this experiment.

Skills Focus Practicing Lab Techniques, Making Observations, Analyzing Data

My Notes

____

____

____

____

____

MODIFICATION FOR GUIDED Inquiry

Provide students with the diagram for this activity and have them use it to build a simple circuit. Supply students with the test materials and have them write out a set of procedures that will allow them to test the conductivity of each material. Have students create a chart in which they will record their observations. Allow students to carry out their investigations, and then encourage students to share their results with the class.

Quick Lab continued

Answer Key

4. Sample answer. The light bulb lights up.

5. Sample answers given below.

Object	Observations	Conductor or insulator?
aluminum foil	light bulb lights up	conductor
craft stick	light bulb does not light	insulator
metal spoon	light bulb lights up	conductor
penny	light bulb lights up brightly	conductor
plastic spoon	light bulb does not light	insulator

6. Sample answer: The aluminum foil, metal spoon, and penny were electrical conductors. The craft stick and plastic spoon were electrical insulators. I know this because the light bulb lit up when the aluminum foil, metal spoon, and penny were attached to the wires. The light bulb did not light with the craft stick and plastic spoon, so they are electrical insulators.
Teacher Prompt What will happen to the light bulb if a material is a conductor? What will happen to the bulb if the material is an insulator?

7. Sample answer: Yes, the copper penny conducted an electric current much better than the spoon. I could tell because the light bulb burned brighter.

8. Sample answer: I think that the metal paperclip would conduct an electric current because all of the metal objects I tested were conductors, while the plastic and wooden objects tested did not conduct an electric current.
Teacher Prompt Did you notice a relationship among the materials that conducted an electric current?

QUICK LAB DIRECTED Inquiry

Investigate Conductors and Insulators

In this activity, you will build a simple circuit and use it to test the conductivity of different materials. A circuit is a series of parts through which electric charges flow. Electric charges will flow easily through an electrical conductor. If an electrical insulator is added into a circuit, electric charges will not flow easily.

OBJECTIVES

- Construct a simple circuit.
- Explore conductors and insulators.

MATERIALS

For each student

- aluminum foil
- battery, D-cell
- battery holder
- craft stick
- flashlight bulb with bulb holder
- safety goggles
- spoon, metal
- spoon, plastic
- penny
- wire, insulated copper with alligator clips (3)

PROCEDURE

1. Insert the light bulb into the bulb holder. Attach one end of a wire to one side of the bulb holder and the other end to one side of the battery holder.

2. Attach a second piece of wire to the other side of the bulb holder. Leave the second end free.

3. Attach the third piece of wire to the second side of the battery holder. Leave the other end of the wire free, as shown below:

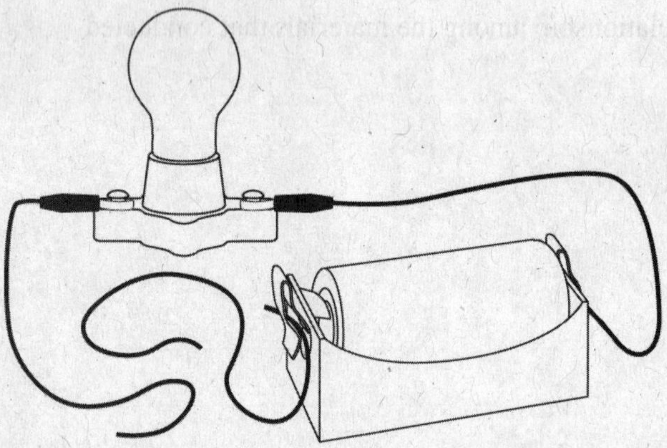

4. Test the light bulb and the battery by touching the free ends of the two wires together. What happens?

____

____

5 Now test the conductivity of each object by attaching the free alligator clips to opposite sides of the object. Record your observations in the table below.

Object	Observations	Conductor or insulator?
aluminum foil		
craft stick		
metal spoon		
penny		
plastic spoon		

6 Which objects were electrical conductors? Which objects were electrical insulators? How can you tell?

____

____

____

____

7 Do any of the conductors seem to conduct an electric current better than the others? Explain.

____

____

____

8 Based on your observations, which of the following objects would most likely conduct an electric current: a plastic cup, a wooden block, or a metal paper clip? Explain your reasoning.

____

____

____

____

QUICK LAB DIRECTED Inquiry

Investigate Electric Current GENERAL

Small groups
30 minutes

LAB RATINGS LESS ← → MORE

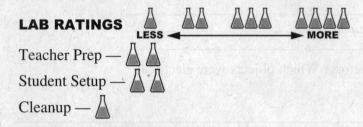

Teacher Prep — 2
Student Setup — 2
Cleanup — 1

MATERIALS

For each group
- batteries, AA 1.5 V, in holder (4)
- bulbs, flashlight, 6.3 V/150 mA, in base (3)
- multimeter
- wire, insulated with alligator clips (4)

For each student
- gloves
- safety goggles

SAFETY INFORMATION

Remind students to review all safety cautions and icons before beginning this lab. Students should wear goggles and hand protection in case of battery failure and leakage. Caution students not to measure the "short circuit" current of a circuit with no bulbs as they may damage the multimeter.

TEACHER NOTES

In this activity, students will work in small groups to construct a series circuit including one to three light bulbs, and use a multimeter to observe the current.

First, the students will construct a series circuit including one light bulb, noting its brightness. Next, they will use the multimeter to measure the current between each of the circuit elements; it should be the same in each place. If you do not have enough multimeters for each student group, check with a high school physics teacher.

Then, the students will check and measure the current with two bulbs, and again with three bulbs.

Tip This lab reinforces the concept that the flow of charge remains the same through a series circuit as it passes through loads.

Skills Focus Practicing Lab Techniques, Making Observations

My Notes

____

____

____

____

MODIFICATION FOR GUIDED Inquiry

Provide the students with the same materials as in the Directed Inquiry activity. Ensure that they know how to measure current in a circuit with the multimeter. Direct them to develop a plan for investigating current in different parts of the circuit. Approve the plan before they begin experimenting.

Quick Lab continued

Answer Key

3. Accept all reasonable answers.
4. Accept all reasonable answers.
5. Accept all reasonable answers.
6. The brightness of the bulbs decreased as more were added.
7. The current decreased as more bulbs were added to the circuit.
8. Within this circuit, the bulbs all had the same brightness.
9. Within each circuit, all the segments had almost the same measured current.
10. Increasing the resistance in the series circuit has the effect of decreasing the measured current.
11. Sample answer: The rate of the flow of charges (the current) is the same in different parts of a series circuit.

Name ______________________ Class ______________ Date ______________

QUICK LAB DIRECTED Inquiry

Investigate Electric Current

Current is the rate of flow of moving charges, measured in amperes. In this activity, you will use light bulbs and a multimeter to measure the current in different parts of three direct current (DC) series circuits.

OBJECTIVES

- Observe the effect of varying the number of light bulbs in the circuit.
- Observe current in different parts of series circuits using a multimeter.

MATERIALS

For each group
- batteries, AA 1.5 V, in holder (4)
- bulbs, flashlight, 6.3 V/150 mA, in base (3)
- multimeter
- wire, insulated with alligator clips (4)

For each student
- gloves
- safety goggles

PROCEDURE

1. Construct the series DC circuit shown below using the batteries, one bulb in a base, and two wire test leads. The light bulb should light. Note the brightness of the bulb and note that this is an example of brightness level "10" on a scale of 1 to 10.

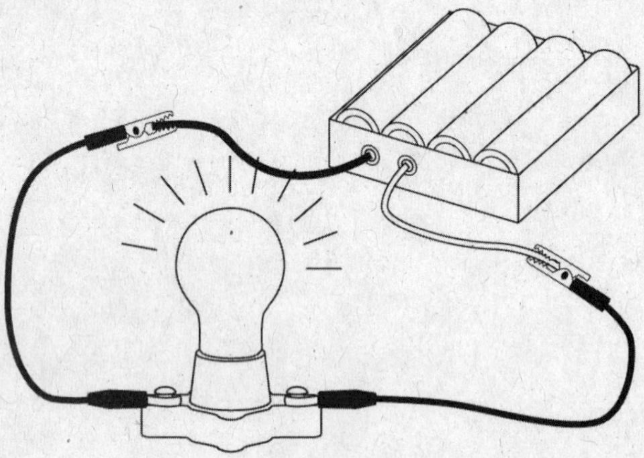

2. Make sure the multimeter is set up to measure current. While making the measurements in the following steps, touch the red test probe to the side of the circuit closest to the battery holder's red wire, and the black probe to the black wire's side.

Quick Lab continued

❸ To measure current, the meter will be included in series in the circuit. Leave the alligator clips attached to the battery holder wires. Use the clip at the other end of one wire to place the multimeter in the circuit between the batteries and the light bulb, as shown in the diagram below. Complete the circuit by touching the test probe to the bulb base. Repeat on the other side of the light bulb. Record your observations in the table below.

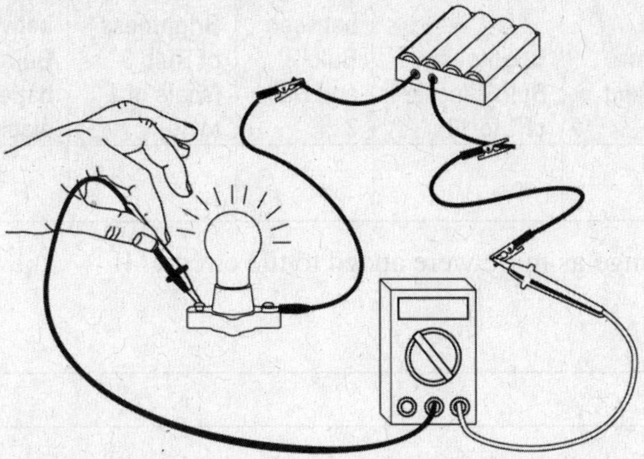

CURRENT IN ONE-BULB CIRCUIT

Current between batteries' red wire and Bulb 1	Brightness of Bulb 1 (scale of 1 to 10)	Current between Bulb 1 and batteries' black wire

❹ Next, include another light bulb, Bulb 2, in series in the circuit. Leaving the alligator clips attached to the battery holder, use the multimeter to measure the current in each segment of the circuit. Note the brightness of each bulb. Record your observations in the table below.

CURRENT IN TWO-BULB CIRCUIT

Current between batteries' red wire and Bulb 1	Brightness of Bulb 1 (scale of 1 to 10)	Current between Bulb 1 and Bulb 2	Brightness of Bulb 2 (scale of 1 to 10)	Current between Bulb 2 and batteries' black wire

Quick Lab continued

5. Finally, include a third light bulb, Bulb 3, in the series circuit. Again, use the multimeter to find the current in each segment and note the brightness of each bulb.

CURRENT IN THREE-BULB CIRCUIT

Current between batteries' red wire and Bulb 1	Brightness of Bulb 1 (scale of 1 to 10)	Current between Bulb 1 and Bulb 2	Brightness of Bulb 2 (scale of 1 to 10)	Current between Bulb 2 and Bulb 3	Brightness of Bulb 3 (scale of 1 to 10)	Current between Bulb 3 and batteries' black wire

6. Did the brightness of the bulbs change as more were added to the circuit? If so, in what way?

____

____

7. Did the current change as more light bulbs were added to the circuit? If so, in what way?

____

____

8. Compare the brightness of the three bulbs in the three-bulb circuit.

____

____

9. Compare the current in different segments in the three-bulb circuit.

____

____

10. Light bulbs provide electrical resistance. What can you infer about the relationship between resistance and current?

____

____

____

11. Based on your observations, describe the flow of charges in different parts of a series circuit.

____

____

____

QUICK LAB DIRECTED Inquiry

Lemon Battery GENERAL

Small groups
20 minutes

LAB RATINGS

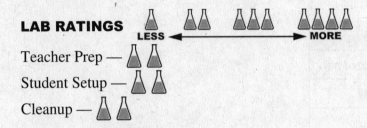

LESS ⟷ MORE

Teacher Prep — 2
Student Setup — 2
Cleanup — 2

MATERIALS

For each group

- calculator, clock, or timer, liquid crystal display (LCD), button cell powered
- knife, plastic
- lemons, fresh (3)
- paper clips, steel (3)
- pennies, pre-1982 (3)
- wire, insulated with alligator clips (4)

For each student

- safety goggles

SAFETY INFORMATION

Remind students to review all safety cautions and icons before beginning this lab. Goggles are recommended to protect eyes from lemon juice, squirted or rubbed from fingers. If nails are used as suggested in the Modification procedure, instruct students to use caution when they push the nails into the lemons. Have paper towels available to clean up lemon juice drippings.

TEACHER NOTES

In this activity, students will build simple batteries out of lemons and use them to run an inexpensive LCD-display calculator, timer, clock, or other device that is normally powered by a button battery. Items powered by other kinds of batteries may not work because the current requirements may be too high. When selecting LCD items, ensure that the battery compartment is accessible. Inexpensive suitable items can be found in thrift shops and "dollar" stores.

Students will roll the lemons on the table to break up the interior membranes. Then they will use the knife to make two 1-cm slits in the rind, about 3 cm apart. They will insert a penny halfway into one hole and a steel paper clip into the other. Then they will use the wire leads to connect the lemons in series to each other and to the LCD item. They may need to hold the wire leads in place on the item if there are no suitable attachment points. The item should operate; they may need to switch the polarity of the leads if it doesn't work the first time.

Use older U.S. pennies for this lab. Pennies minted before 1982 contain much more copper and work better than those minted in 1983 or later.

To save lab time, prepare the LCD devices in advance. For each device, install a battery to be sure the device works. Then remove the battery and place opaque tape over any solar cells. Set the battery compartment cover aside and leave the battery compartment open.

Tip Although cups of lemon juice work at least as well as lemons for this lab, it captures students' imaginations to construct a working battery in an appealing self-contained "package" similar to their familiar AA and other commercial batteries.

My Notes

Quick Lab continued

Student Tip Think about where the power in batteries comes from.

Skills Focus Making Observations, Building Models

MODIFICATION FOR GUIDED *Inquiry*

Provide the students with the materials necessary to build the battery, as well as other items to try in various combinations. Ideas for materials:

Battery body	Cathode	Anode
apple	pre-1982 penny	galvanized nail
lemon	post-1982 penny	iron nail
potato	thick copper wire	paper clip

Explain the general idea of inserting two items into a fruit or vegetable and measuring the voltage and current produced, if any, using a multimeter. Before they build anything, instruct students to plan a series of experiments to use the provided materials to find the best combination for voltage and current production. When the best combination has been determined, provide the LCD devices to be powered.

Another interesting option is to provide a flashlight bulb in a base and a red LED in addition to the LCD item. Students may be surprised that even several lemons cannot operate a flashlight bulb, and that even an LED light only lights dimly with three or four lemons, but that LCD calculators, timers, or clocks—seemingly more "active" devices—run well.

Answer Key

7. Sample answer: Our calculator powered on. We were able to get it to perform calculations.
8. Sample answer: When the lemons were connected in a chain, we were able to get more electrical energy.
9. Sample answer: When the lemons and the LCD device were connected, electric charges could flow.

QUICK LAB DIRECTED Inquiry

Lemon Battery

Batteries have the ability to convert chemical energy into electrical energy, which can be used to power devices such as cars, flashlights, and electronics. Usually, we buy manufactured batteries for these purposes. In this activity, you will use common materials to make and use a working battery.

OBJECTIVE

- Build batteries from lemons and use the energy to run an everyday device.

MATERIALS

For each group

- calculator, clock, or timer, liquid crystal display (LCD), button cell powered
- knife, plastic
- lemons, fresh (3)
- paper clips, steel (3)
- pennies, pre-1982 (3)
- wire, insulated, with alligator clips (4)

For each student

- safety goggles

PROCEDURE

1. Gently press down on the lemons with the palm of your hand and roll them around on your desk. Do not crush the lemons.
2. Use the plastic knife to make two 1-cm (centimeter) slits in each lemon's rind, about 3 cm apart. Cut through the rind and down into the fruit.
3. In each lemon, insert a penny into one slit and a paper clip into the other. Push each object in at least halfway.
4. Use the wire leads to connect the lemons in a chain. Connect the paper clip of one to the penny in another lemon. On the lemon at one end, there should be a wire lead connected to a paper clip. On the lemon at the other end, a lead should be connected to a penny.
5. Examine the battery compartment of the LCD device. If possible, attach the two wire leads from the lemons at each end to the positive and negative battery terminals. Otherwise, hold them in place. Make sure the wire leads do not touch each other.

Name ______________________ Class ______________ Date ______________

Quick Lab continued

6. Attempt to power on the device and to change the display by setting the time or doing a calculation. If it does not work, try these things:

   - Check that the leads connecting the lemons are attached to a paperclip or the LCD device at one end, and a penny or the LCD device at the other.
   - Switch the positions of the wire leads in the device.
   - Borrow another lemon battery cell from another group and add it into your chain.

7. Did your LCD device power on? Were you able to get it to work?

   ____

   ____

8. Why were the lemons connected to one another in a chain?

   ____

   ____

9. Describe the flow of charges in a working lemon battery setup.

   ____

   ____

   ____

S.T.E.M. LAB DIRECTED *Inquiry* **AND** GUIDED *Inquiry*

Voltage, Current, and Resistance

GENERAL

Small groups
45 minutes

LAB RATINGS

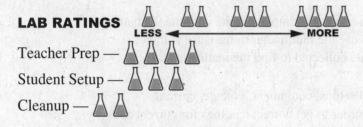

LESS ⟷ MORE

Teacher Prep —

Student Setup —

Cleanup —

MATERIALS

For each group
- battery, 9V
- calculator
- multimeter, digital, with test leads
- pencil pieces, cut and sharpened on both ends (3, various lengths)
- ruler, metric
- wire, insulated with alligator clips (2)

For each student
- gloves
- safety goggles

SAFETY INFORMATION

Remind students to review all safety cautions and icons before beginning this lab. Be sure that the students do not create a short circuit across the 9V battery terminals by connecting the wires without a resistor between them, or by touching the ends together. Students should wear goggles and hand protection because of the possibility of battery failure and leakage.

TEACHER NOTES

In this activity, students will explore the electrical relationship $V = IR$, where V is voltage in volts, I is current in amperes, and R is resistance in ohms. They will test pencil lead resistors in a simple DC circuit.

For the directed inquiry, before the activity, introduce students to the relationship, $V = IR$. Reinforce the concepts of voltage, current, and resistance. Explain that they will be demonstrating the validity of this relationship. For the guided inquiry, explain that there is a simple mathematical relationship connecting voltage, current, and resistance, but do not give the formula. Explain that by analyzing the data from the lab, they will be able to discover this relationship.

If the students are not already familiar with the use of a multimeter, you may wish to conduct a tutorial on their use and provide a reference handout for each group with any equipment-specific settings or cautions. Approximate range values required for this lab will be 0–10 V (volts) DC, 0.1 to 1 A (ampere), and 5–20 Ω (ohms).

Be sure that all the pencils are the same hardness (e.g., #2) and from the same manufacturer for consistency of core diameter and graphite/binder composition. Standard graphite pencils have about 17 cm of wood-covered graphite. Cut off the eraser end and sharpen both ends of the pencils. Make enough pieces so that each group can have a short (about 6 cm), a medium, and a long piece. Make a few extra in case of broken leads. The graphite in some pencils fractures easily. Therefore, first make one or two pencil pieces and attach the alligator clips to the pencil leads to make sure that the lead is strong enough. Be sure that students recognize that the "lead" in a regular #2 pencil is actually graphite mixed with a binder such as a polymer or clay.

My Notes

S.T.E.M. Lab continued

For the Directed Inquiry, students will construct a simple circuit with the 9V battery in series with one pencil piece at a time. Using the multimeter, for each piece, they will measure the voltage drop across the pencil piece, the current in the circuit, and the piece's resistance and enter the results in a table. If you do not have enough multimeters for each student group, check with a high school physics teacher. The students will calculate the values for the pencils' resistance from the measured values of voltage and current, and compare the percentage difference with the resistances measured by the meter to confirm the formula.

For the Guided Inquiry, instruct students to construct simple circuits with the 9V battery in series with one pencil piece at a time and to use the multimeter to measure voltage, current, resistance. Guide them in using the data collected to find the mathematical relationship.

Tip This lab can serve as practice in electrical setups, equipment, voltage, current, resistance, and mathematical relationships. In order to get correct readings for current and resistance, students should be sure that they have constructed their circuit as a series circuit.

Skills Focus Practicing Lab Techniques, Collecting Data, Drawing Conclusions

MODIFICATION FOR INDEPENDENT Inquiry

Ensure that students know how to connect a simple DC series circuit and use the multimeter to measure voltage, current, and resistance. Provide the same materials as for the Directed and Guided Labs. Explain that the pencil leads can be used as resistors. Allow students to develop their own plan to use the materials to discover a relationship between voltage, current, and resistance.

Answer Key for DIRECTED Inquiry

MAKE OBSERVATIONS

2. Accept all reasonable answers.

4. Accept all reasonable answers.

5. Accept all reasonable answers.

6. Accept all reasonable answers.

7. Accept all reasonable answers.

ANALYZE THE RESULTS

8. Accept all reasonable answers.

9. Accept all reasonable answers.

DRAW CONCLUSIONS

10. Sample answer: The percent differences were all under 10%, so the data do support the formula.

S.T.E.M. Lab continued

11. The calculated value comes from the theory, and the measured value comes from actual measurements. There could be measurement or calculation error, or there may be other sources of resistance in the circuit, like the wires.

Connect TO THE ESSENTIAL QUESTION

12. Sample answer: The rate of charge flow (current) depends on the voltage and the resistance.

13. Sample answer: The voltage and the current are related to the resistance.

Answer Key for GUIDED Inquiry

MAKE OBSERVATIONS

2. Accept all reasonable answers.

4. Accept all reasonable answers.

5. Accept all reasonable answers.

6. Accept all reasonable answers.

7. Accept all reasonable answers.

ANALYZE THE RESULTS

8. $V = IR$ or $I = \dfrac{V}{R}$ or $R = \dfrac{V}{I}$

Teacher Prompt Take the values for voltage, current, and resistance from one of your trials. Can you take two of them and divide or multiply them together so that you get the third number? If you find a way that works, does it also work for the sets of numbers in the other two trials?

9. The calculated value comes from the theory, and the measured value comes from actual measurements. There could be measurement or calculation error, or there may be other sources of resistance in the circuit, like the wires.

Connect TO THE ESSENTIAL QUESTION

10. Sample answer: The rate of charge flow (current) depends on the voltage and the resistance.

11. Sample answer: The voltage and the current are related to the resistance.

Name ______________________ Class ______________ Date ____________________

S.T.E.M. LAB DIRECTED *Inquiry*

Voltage, Current, and Resistance

Voltage, current, and resistance in a circuit can be measured using a multimeter. These three properties are mathematically related by the formula $V = IR$, where V is the voltage in volts, I is the current in amperes, and R is the resistance in ohms. In this activity, you will use measurements from circuits to confirm this relationship.

OBJECTIVES

- Build simple circuits and use a multimeter to collect data about them.
- Use data to confirm the mathematical relationship among voltage, current, and resistance.

MATERIALS

For each group
- battery, 9V
- calculator
- multimeter, digital, with test leads
- pencil pieces, cut and sharpened on both ends (3, various lengths)
- ruler, metric
- wire, insulated, with alligator clips (2)

For each student
- gloves
- safety goggles

PROCEDURE

MAKE OBSERVATIONS

1 You will build some circuits to test the formula $V=IR$. In these circuits, you will use the pencil leads as the source of resistance. (Hint: "Lead" in a regular #2 pencil isn't really lead; it's graphite mixed with a binder such as a polymer or clay.)

You will measure the voltage and the current in the circuit when a pencil is included. You will then use the formula to calculate the resistance, R_{calc} ,of each the pencil. You will also measure the resistance, R_{meas}, of each pencil when it is not part of the circuit. You will then compare R_{meas} with R_{calc} to confirm the formula. You will record your measurements in a data table such as the one shown below.

MEASURED AND CALCULATED RESISTANCES OF PENCIL LEAD PIECES

Pencil length, cm	Voltage (V) across pencil, volts	Current (I), amps	Measured resistance (R_{meas}), ohms	Calculated resistance (R_{calc}), ohms	Percent difference between R_{calc} and R_{meas}

2 Use the ruler to measure the lengths in centimeters (cm) of each of the pencil pieces from tip to tip. Enter the values into the data table.

3. Set up the test circuit to include a pencil as in the diagram below.
It is important to connect the clip only to the graphite and not to the wood.

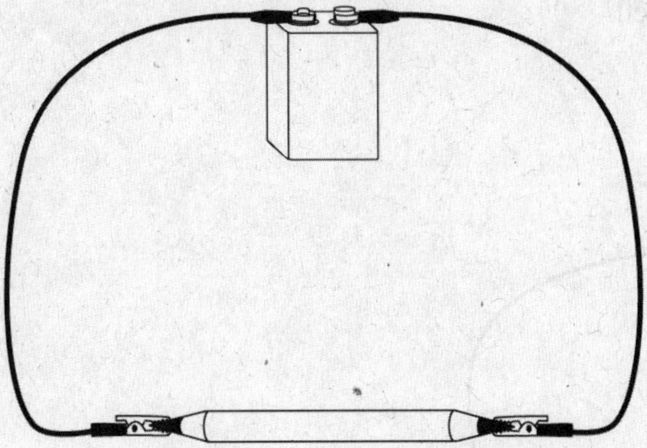

4. Resistance in a circuit reduces the voltage of the electricity as it goes through the circuit. Measure the voltage (V).

a. Set up the multimeter to test for DC voltage.
b. For a good connection, firmly touch the multimeter leads to the alligator clips (not the graphite) on the pencil. The red test lead goes on the clip attached to the positive (+) side of the battery.
c. Record your result in the data table to the nearest hundredth of a volt. Leave the alligator clips attached to the pencil in place.

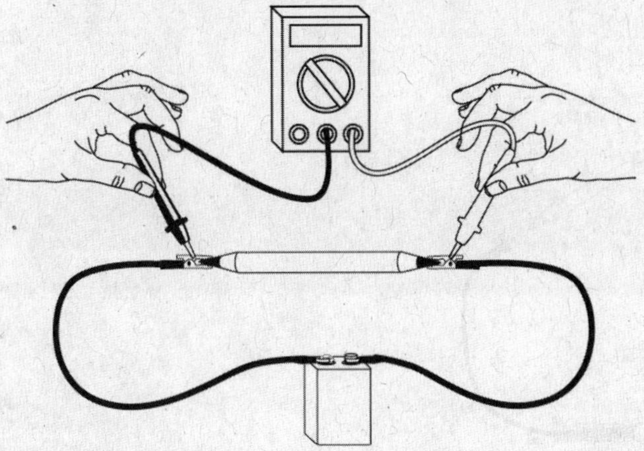

5. Measure the current (I) in the circuit.

a. Set up the multimeter to measure current in amps.
b. Remove the wire clip from the positive terminal of the battery and attach the clip to the black multimeter lead. Touch the red multimeter lead to the positive battery terminal. This makes the meter part of the circuit, and electric charges will flow through both the pencil and the meter.

c. Record the value for the current in your data table. Round to the nearest hundredth of an amp. (Hint: Convert from mA to A if necessary by dividing by 1000.) Leave the alligator clips attached to the pencil.

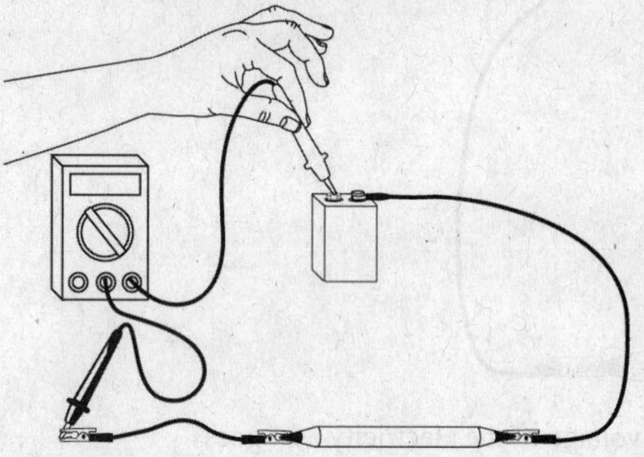

6 Measure the resistance (R_{meas}) of the pencil piece. Notice that you are measuring the resistance of the pencil when it is not part of the circuit.

a. Set up the multimeter to measure resistance in ohms.
b. Disconnect the clips from the battery and connect them to the multimeter test leads.
c. Record the value for the pencil piece resistance in the data table, rounding to the nearest tenth of an ohm.

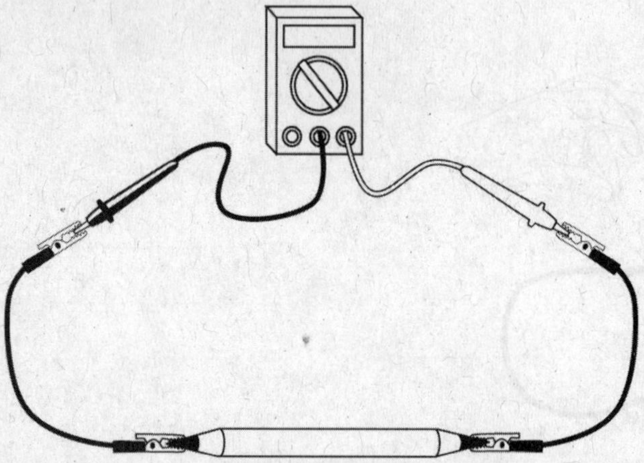

7 Repeat Steps 2–5 for the other two pencil pieces.

ANALYZE THE RESULTS

8 **Examining Evidence** To find R_{calc}, you will use the $V = IR$ formula. Rearrange the formula to solve for R.

$$R_{calc} = \frac{V}{I}$$

If the formula $V=IR$ is valid, then the R_{calc} values should closely match the R_{meas} values. Using the formula above, calculate the expected value R_{calc} for each pencil resistor and enter it in the table.

9 **Evaluating Data** For each pencil piece, find the percent difference between R_{calc} and R_{meas} using this formula.

$$\% \text{ difference} = \frac{(R_{calc} - R_{meas})}{(R_{meas})} \times 100$$

DRAW CONCLUSIONS

10 **Interpreting Observations** Were the percent differences between the measured and the calculated resistances large or small? What do you conclude about the validity of the $V = IR$ formula?

____

____

11 **Applying Concepts** What do you think caused the differences, if any, between your measured and your calculated resistance values?

____

____

____

Connect **TO THE ESSENTIAL QUESTION**

12 **Applying Concepts** Describe the relationship between voltage and resistance.

____

____

13 **Applying Concepts** Describe the relationship between voltage and current.

____

____

Name ______________________ Class ______________ Date ______________

S.T.E.M. LAB GUIDED Inquiry

Voltage, Current, and Resistance

Voltage, current, and resistance in a circuit can be measured using a multimeter. These three properties are mathematically related by a simple formula. In this activity, you will use measurements from circuits to determine this relationship.

PROCEDURE

MAKE OBSERVATIONS

1. The formula $V = IR$ can be used to find resistance values in a circuit. You will build some circuits to test the formula. In these circuits, you will use the pencil leads as the source of resistance. ("Lead" in a regular #2 pencil isn't really lead; it's graphite mixed with a binder such as a polymer or clay.)

   You will measure the voltage and the current in the circuit when a pencil is included. You will also measure the resistance, R, of each pencil when they are not part of the circuit. Prepare a table such as the one below to record your data.

CIRCUIT DATA

Pencil length, cm	Voltage (V) across pencil, volts	Current (I), amps	Resistance (R), ohms

2. Use the ruler to measure the lengths in centimeters of each of the pencil pieces from tip to tip. Enter the values into the data table.

OBJECTIVES

- Build simple circuits and use a multimeter to collect data about them.
- Use data to confirm the mathematical relationship among voltage, current, and resistance.

MATERIALS

For each group

- battery, 9V
- calculator
- multimeter, digital, with test leads and optional instructional handout
- pencil pieces, cut and sharpened on both ends (3, various lengths)
- ruler, metric
- wire, insulated, with alligator clips (2)

For each student

- gloves
- safety goggles

3 Set up the test circuit to include a pencil as in the diagram below. Connect one terminal of the battery to one end of the shortest pencil, and the other terminal to the other end. It is important to connect the clip only to the graphite and not to the wood.

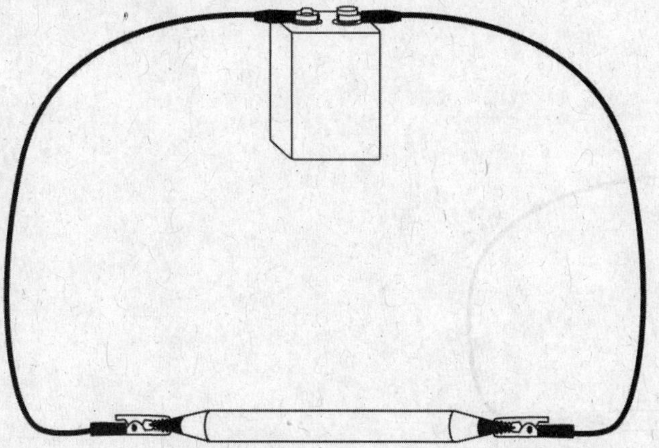

4 Resistance in a circuit reduces the voltage of the electricity as it goes through the circuit. Measure the voltage drop, *V*, across the pencil.

a. Set up the multimeter to test for DC voltage.
b. Firmly touch the multimeter leads to the alligator clips on the pencil. The red test lead goes on the clip attached to the positive (+) side of the battery.
c. Record your result in the data table to the nearest hundredth of a volt. Leave the alligator clips attached to the pencil in place.

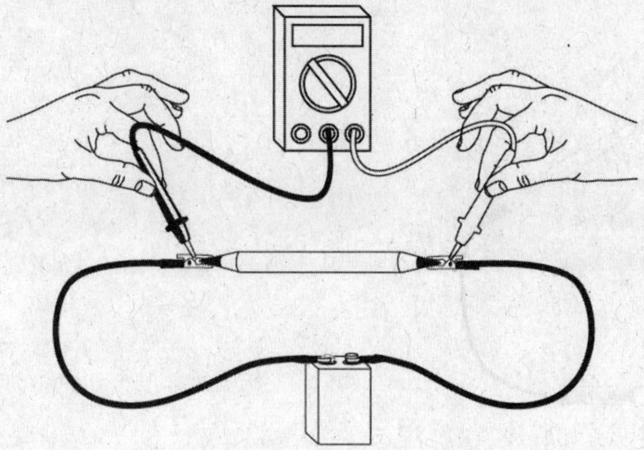

5 Measure the current, *I*, in the circuit.

a. Set up the multimeter to measure current in amps.
b. Remove the wire clip on the positive terminal of the battery and attach the clip to the black multimeter lead. Touch the red multimeter lead to the positive battery terminal. This makes the meter part of the circuit, and electric charges will flow through both the pencil and the meter.

S.T.E.M. Lab continued

c. Record the value for the current in your data table. Round to the nearest hundredth of an amp. (Hint: Convert from mA to A if necessary by dividing by 1000.) Leave the alligator clips attached to the pencil.

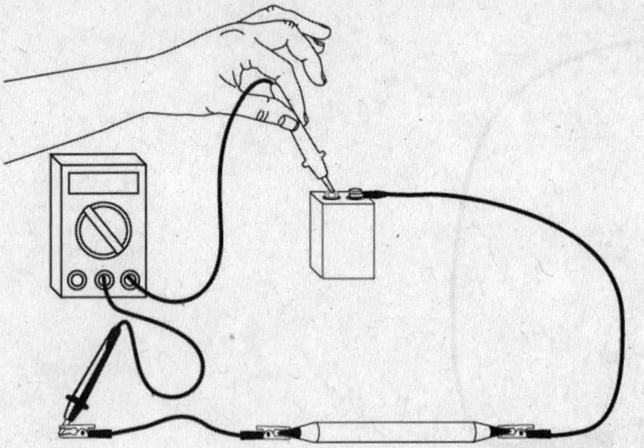

6 Measure the resistance, *R*, of the pencil piece. Notice that you are measuring the resistance of the pencil when it is not part of the circuit.

a. Set up the multimeter to measure resistance in ohms.
b. Disconnect the clips from the battery and connect them to the multimeter test leads.
c. Record the value for the pencil piece resistance in the data table, rounding to the nearest tenth of an ohm.

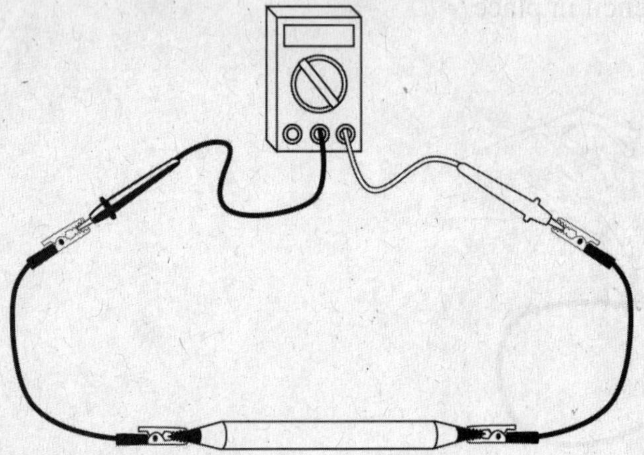

7 Repeat Steps 2–5 for the other two pencil pieces.

ANALYZE THE RESULTS

8 **Interpreting Data** Look in your data table at the values *V*, *I*, and *R*. Try to discover a formula that relates all three of these quantities. Take values two at a time and multiply or divide them, and compare the result with the third. Your formula should work fairly well with all three sets of data, but the numbers probably won't come out exactly the same. Write your formula here:

____

9 **Applying Concepts** What do you think caused the differences, if any, between your measured and your calculated resistance values?

____

____

____

Connect TO THE ESSENTIAL QUESTION

10 **Applying Concepts** Describe the relationship between voltage and resistance.

____

____

11 **Applying Concepts** Describe the relationship between voltage and current.

____

____

QUICK LAB GUIDED Inquiry

Compare Parallel and Series Circuits GENERAL

Small groups
20 minutes

LAB RATINGS LESS ◄——► MORE

Teacher Prep — 1 flask
Student Setup — 2 flasks
Cleanup — 2 flasks

MATERIALS

For each group
- battery, D–cell, in holder
- light bulb, with holder (2)
- wire, insulated with alligator clips (4)

For each student
- safety goggles

My Notes

SAFETY INFORMATION

Remind students to review all safety cautions and icons before beginning this lab. Caution students not to touch any non-insulated pieces of wire while the circuit is connected to the battery.

TEACHER NOTES

In this activity, students will construct series and parallel circuits and observe the brightness of light bulbs in each circuit. Students will draw conclusions about the voltage across elements in series and parallel circuits.

Student Tip Pay particular attention to the brightness of the light bulbs in each circuit. How does the brightness compare?

Skills Focus Comparing Observations

MODIFICATION FOR DIRECTED Inquiry

Direct students through each step of the process as they construct the circuits. For the series circuit, have students connect a wire from the positive terminal of the battery holder to one end of the first light bulb. Then, they should connect another wire from the second end of the first light bulb to the first end of a second light bulb. Finally, they will connect a wire from the second end of the second light bulb to the negative terminal of the battery holder. For the parallel circuit, students will need four wires. They should connect the first wire from the positive terminal of the battery holder to one end of the first light bulb. Then, they should connect the second wire from the same end of the first light bulb to one end of the second light bulb. Have students repeat this process for the other side of the circuit. (Students should connect a wire from the negative battery terminal to the second end of the first light bulb, and then should connect another wire from the second end of the first light bulb to the second end of the second light bulb.) Have students make and record observations of the light bulbs in both circuits, and have them use their observations to compare and contrast the two circuits.

Quick Lab continued

Answer Key

2. Accept all reasonable answers.

4. Accept all reasonable answers. The observations should indicate that the light from bulbs in this circuit was very bright.

5. Sample answer: The two light bulbs were brighter with the parallel circuit.

6. Sample answer: The light bulbs receive the most voltage in the parallel circuit.

7. Sample answer: This statement describes the parallel circuit because the light bulbs emitted the most light in this circuit. Also, because there are multiple paths around which current flows, the current divides up through the different paths.

8. Sample answer: This statement describes the series circuit because the light bulbs were dimmer in this circuit. This indicates that the voltage was divided between the two light bulbs. However, because the current flows through one loop, the current remains the same through the entire circuit.

Name ______________________ Class ______________ Date ______________

QUICK LAB GUIDED *Inquiry*

Compare Parallel and Series Circuits

In this lab, you will build a series circuit and parallel circuit. Then, you will compare the brightness of light bulbs in both circuits and draw conclusions about the voltage in each circuit.

OBJECTIVES

- Construct series and parallel circuits.
- Compare voltage across elements in series and parallel circuits.

MATERIALS

For each group
- battery, D-cell, in holder
- light bulb, with holder (2)
- wire, insulated with alligator clips (4)

For each student
- safety goggles

PROCEDURE

1. Construct a series circuit that resembles the diagram below:

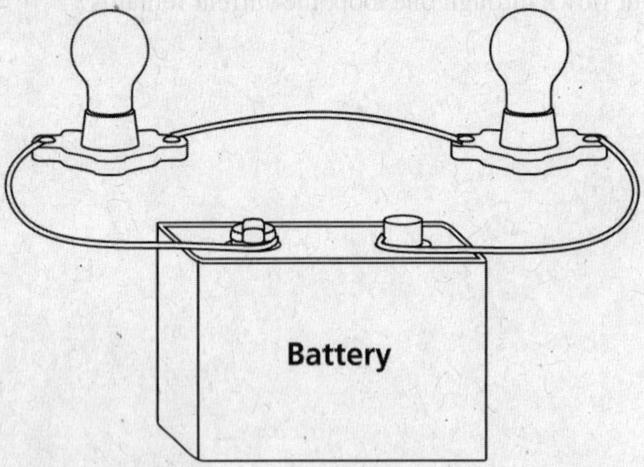

2. When the circuit is complete, observe the light bulbs and record your observations.

____

____

3. Construct a parallel circuit that resembles the diagram below:

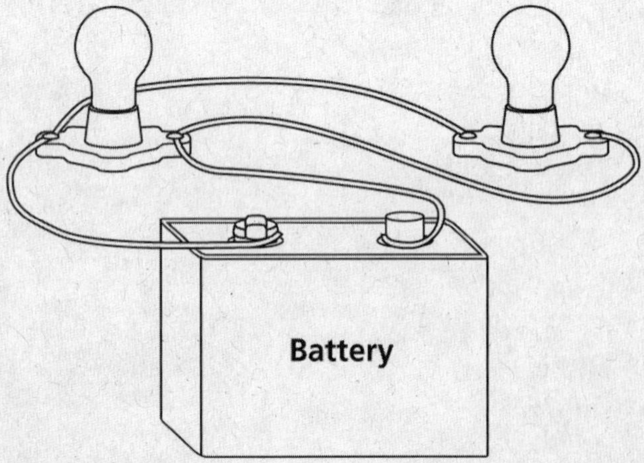

Quick Lab continued

4. Observe the light bulbs in the parallel circuit and record your observations.

____

____

5. In which circuit did the bulbs emit more light?

____

6. The amount of voltage that each light bulb receives determines how brightly it shines. In which circuit do the light bulbs receive the most voltage?

____

7. In some circuits, each light bulb in the circuit receives the full voltage from the battery, but the current through the circuit is divided up. Which circuit in this investigation does this statement describe? Explain your reasoning.

____

____

____

8. In some circuits, each light bulb in the circuit receives a portion of the voltage from the battery, but the current is the same throughout the circuit. Which circuit in this investigation does this statement describe? Explain your reasoning.

____

____

____

QUICK LAB DIRECTED *Inquiry*

Compare Materials for Use in Fuses GENERAL

Small groups
30 minutes

LAB RATINGS

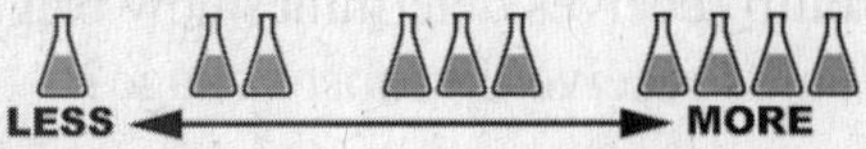

Teacher Prep — 

Student Setup — 

Cleanup — 

MATERIALS

For each group

- battery, 6V
- jar, clear glass
- steel wool, single strand
- stopwatch
- tape, duct
- wire, bare copper
- wire, insulated with alligator clips (2)

For each student

- gloves
- lab apron
- safety goggles

My Notes

SAFETY INFORMATION

Remind students to review all safety cautions and icons before beginning this lab. This activity may result in noxious fumes. Ensure that there is adequate ventilation in the classroom and instruct students to keep their faces away from the jar. Also, remind students to wear goggles at all times.

TEACHER NOTES

In this activity, students will explore conductors and insulators by inserting different materials into an electric circuit and observing the time it takes for each material to melt. A jar should be used as a safety chamber so that the materials inserted into the circuit will melt inside the jar. Students will observe that steel wool melts whereas copper will not. They should use this data to conclude that steel wool has greater electrical resistance and thus is a more ideal material for use in a fuse. The steel wool is likely not just to melt, but also to momentarily glow red before it breaks the circuit. While this is not a safety issue, it might alarm students, so warn them of this beforehand.

For comparison purposes, it is important to use copper wire of the same gauge as the steel wool. Copper wool or copper mesh of a gauge similar to that of steel wool can be purchased in hardware stores and stores specializing in home building, renovation, and repair.

Tip This activity will help the student understand that circuit breakers and fuses are devices designed to "break" an electrical circuit when the current gets too high.

Student Tip Why is copper most commonly used for electrical wiring?

Skills Focus Comparing Observations, Drawing Conclusions

MODIFICATION GUIDED *Inquiry*

For the Guided Inquiry option provide students with the materials listed and procedure for comparing steel and copper in a circuit. Have students share their results and draw conclusions about which material would be more ideal for use in a fuse.

Quick Lab continued

Answer Key

4. Accept all reasonable answers.
   Teacher Prompt What happens when too much electric current passes through a material?
5. Accept all reasonable answers. The strand of steel wool melts, whereas a strand of copper of the same dimensions will not.
6. Accept all reasonable answers.
7. Sample answer: The steel would make a better fuse because it would break an overloaded circuit more quickly.
   Teacher Prompt What is the function of a fuse?

Name ______________________________ Class ________________ Date ________________________

QUICK LAB DIRECTED Inquiry

Compare Materials for Use in Fuses

In this lab you will pass electric current through two different materials to compare their suitability for use as a fuse. Remember that when electric currents in a circuit are too high, they can cause wires to heat to dangerously high temperatures. Fuses are designed to melt and break a circuit when the current in a circuit is too high.

OBJECTIVE

- Determine the best material to use for a fuse.

MATERIALS

- battery, 6V
- jar, clear glass
- steel wool, single strand
- stopwatch
- tape, duct
- wire, bare copper
- wire, insulated with alligator clips (2)

For each student

- gloves
- lab apron
- safety goggles

PROCEDURE

1. Use the alligator clips to clip one end of each wire to the steel wool strand. You can bend and double the ends of the wire if you find it difficult to clip the alligator clips to the wire.

2. Place the steel wool strand in the jar. Tape the wires to the sides of the jar.

3. Clip the free end of one wire to the negative terminal of the battery.

4. What do you predict will happen when you complete the circuit?

   ____

   ____

5. Clip the free end of the remaining wire to the positive terminal of the battery and begin the stopwatch. Observe the steel wool strand and determine the time it takes for the steel wool to melt completely. Record this data in the table below.

	Observations
Steel wool strand	
Copper wire	

6. Repeat Steps 1 through 4 with the copper wire. Write your prediction below. Then carry out the experiment and record your observations in the table above.

   ____

   ____

Quick Lab continued

7. Which material would make a better fuse? Explain your reasoning.

____

____

____

EXPLORATION LAB GUIDED *Inquiry* **AND** INDEPENDENT *Inquiry*

Model the Electric Circuits in a Room GENERAL

Small groups
Two 45-minute class periods

LAB RATINGS (LESS ← → MORE)

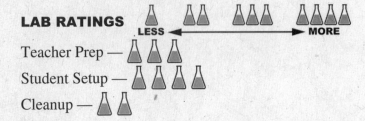

Teacher Prep — 3 flasks
Student Setup — 4 flasks
Cleanup — 2 flasks

MATERIALS

For each group
- batteries, Type D, with holders (2)
- light bulbs, small, with holders (3)
- paper
- shoe box
- switches (3)
- tape, electrical
- tape, transparent
- wire cutter
- wire, insulated

For each student
- lab apron
- safety goggles

My Notes

SAFETY INFORMATION

Remind students to review all safety cautions and icons before beginning this lab. Students are dealing with electricity. Do not use any electrical outlets in conjunction with this activity.

TEACHER NOTES

In this activity, students first use electrical symbols to draw a circuit diagram to communicate circuit layouts in a clear and graphically simple way. Drawing a circuit diagram is an essential precursor to building a real circuit. A key skill is to interpret circuit diagrams and then build a real electric circuit. Students are challenged to ensure that each device is part of a complete circuit that can be controlled with a switch. The students then build the circuit to test their diagram. The student uses materials to simulate the wiring of a typical domestic room. Students use the shoebox to represent a room in a house that includes a ceiling light and two appliances. Conditions stipulate that each appliance must be on a different wall of the room. The light bulbs represent appliances in the diagram. To get students thinking about the appliances and circuits in a room, you may wish to display or pass around pictures of various electrical appliances, ceiling lights, etc.

Tip This activity helps students describe the parts of an electrical circuit, to understand that more than one type of model can represent a system and to use a prototype to test a graphic model.

Student Tip When you switch on one light in a room, why don't all the lights turn on?

Skills Focus Practicing Lab Techniques, Constructing Models, Interpreting Observations

Exploration Lab continued

MODIFICATION FOR DIRECTED Inquiry

For the Directed Inquiry option, present students with two or three example circuits that would meet the requirements for the model. Ask students to explain these and then to create an actual circuit diagram.

Answer Key to GUIDED Inquiry

ASK A QUESTION

1. Sample answer: When you switch on a light in a room, all the lights do not turn on because they are connected to circuits that are controlled by separate switches.
   Teacher prompt What stops electric current from moving around a circuit?
2. Sample answer: A circuit that will only turn on certain appliances will have individual switches to control each appliance.
   Teacher prompt What devices can be used to control appliances individually?

DEVELOP A PLAN

4. Sample answer: For this model, a parallel circuit will work better because we want to connect separate appliances to a single energy source.
   Teacher prompt What would happen if you connected everything to a battery on a series circuit?
5. Sample answer: The additional appliances can be represented with the bulb symbol.
   Teacher prompt What symbols represent items that will be switched on when the circuit is complete?
6. Sample circuit:

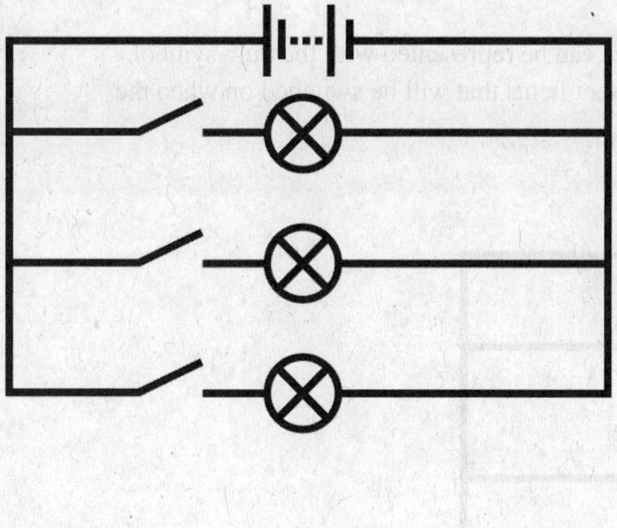

Exploration Lab continued

DRAW CONCLUSIONS

9. Sample answer: No, the circuit did not work as expected because of the location of the switches.
Teacher prompt How did you expect the circuit to work based on your circuit diagram?

10. Sample answer: Yes, we changed the design of the circuit to ensure the switches turned on only one appliance a time.

Connect TO THE ESSENTIAL QUESTION

11. Sample answer: When you close the switch of a circuit, the circuit is complete. This allows electric charges to flow throughout the circuit and provide electrical energy to the appliances.
Teacher prompt What is the source of energy for the appliances?

Answer Key to INDEPENDENT Inquiry

ASK A QUESTION

1. Sample answer: The electrician uses a wiring diagram to plan the circuit.
Teacher prompt What's a better way to build a circuit other than by trial and error?

DEVELOP A PLAN

2. Sample answer: For this circuit, a parallel circuit will work better since we want to connect separate appliances to a single energy source.
Teacher prompt What would happen if you connected everything to a battery on a series circuit?

3. Sample answer: The additional appliances can be represented with the bulb symbol.
Teacher prompt What symbols represent items that will be switched on when the circuit is complete?

4. Sample circuit:

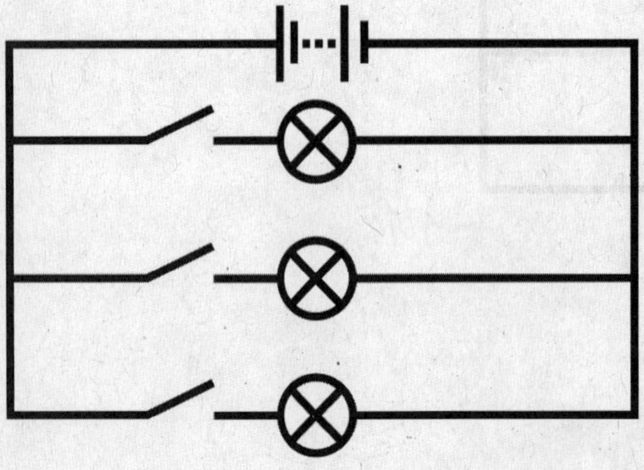

Exploration Lab continued

BUILD A MODEL

5. Sample answer: To represent the source of electrical energy outside the home we can locate the batteries outside the box.
Teacher prompt What is the source of energy and what does the box represent?

DRAW CONCLUSIONS

8. Sample answer: No, the circuit did not work as expected because of the location of the switches.
Teacher prompt How did you expect the circuit to work based on your circuit diagram?

9. Sample answer: Yes, we changed the design of the circuit to ensure the switches turned on only one appliance a time.

Connect TO THE ESSENTIAL QUESTION

10. Sample answer: When you close a switch on the circuit, the circuit is complete. This allows electric charges to flow throughout the circuit and provide electrical energy to the appliances.
Teacher prompt What is the source of energy for the appliances?

Name ______________________ Class ______________ Date ______________________

EXPLORATION LAB GUIDED *Inquiry*

Model the Electric Circuits in a Room

In a typical home, there are many devices that use electrical energy, such as lights, fans, televisions, refrigerators, microwave ovens, and computers. Wall switches control some of these devices. Others have their own built-in switches. In addition, there are wires in a home that supply the electric current needed to run these devices. These wires are typically hidden from view and are often part of a larger circuit with many side branches.

In this lab, you will build a model of a room wired to supply electrical energy from a battery to three different appliances. Your model will include switches that you can use to control the appliances. Before you build your model, you will develop a plan by drawing an electric circuit to simulate your model room with its three appliances and their switches. You will then check the feasibility of your circuit by building the model and testing it.

OBJECTIVES

- Draw an electric circuit that models the lights and appliances in a room.
- Test the circuit by building a model using wire, batteries, and light bulbs.

MATERIALS

- batteries, Type D, with holders (2)
- light bulbs, small, with holders (3)
- paper
- shoe box
- switches (3)
- tape, electrical
- tape, transparent
- wire cutter
- wire, insulated

For each student

- lab apron
- safety goggles

PROCEDURE

ASK A QUESTION

1 When you switch on one light in a room, why don't all the lights turn on?

____

2 How do you create a circuit that will only turn on certain appliances?

____

____

DEVELOP A PLAN

3 You will build a model that meets the following criteria:

- The circuit must model one room of a house that includes a ceiling light and two "appliances."
- Each light or appliance must be on a different wall of the room.
- Each part of the circuit must be activated by a separate switch.
- The circuit must work according to a diagram that you prepare before you build the physical model.

Name ______________________ Class ______________ Date ______________

Exploration Lab continued

4 Talk about the model you will build with other members of your group. Will a series circuit or a parallel circuit work better if you want to wire three appliances that are controlled separately? Explain.

____

____

____

5 A circuit diagram uses symbols to represent the components of the circuit. Because light bulbs are the only devices available, you will use them as stand-ins for "appliances" in your working model. How will you represent the "appliances" in your circuit diagram?

____

6 Work with the other members of your group to draw a circuit diagram on the paper provided. Use the electrical symbol key shown below to represent parts of the circuit diagram as you plan your room. Remember, the circuit must include a ceiling light and two "appliances."

Electric symbol key	
Wire	
Crossed wire (not connected)	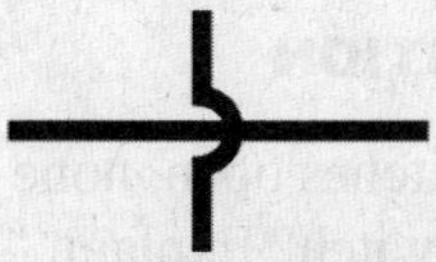
Battery	
Lamp	
Switch	

BUILD A MODEL

7. Use the shoe box to build a physical model of the room you drew. In most homes, the source of electrical energy is outside the home. Build your model so that the batteries are outside the room.

ANALYZE THE RESULTS

8. **Developing Models** Test your design by connecting the batteries. If necessary, change your circuit until it works correctly. If you change your circuit, make the same changes on your circuit diagram.

DRAW CONCLUSIONS

9. **Describing Results** Did your circuit work as expected? Explain.

____

____

____

10. **Evaluating Models** Did you have to make changes to the design of your circuit? Explain.

____

____

____

Connect TO THE ESSENTIAL QUESTION

11. **Explaining Observations** With all switches open, none of the appliances work. What happens when you close a switch? Explain.

____

____

____

Name ________________________ Class ____________ Date ________________

EXPLORATION LAB INDEPENDENT *Inquiry*

Model the Electric Circuits in a Room

In a typical home, there are many devices that use electrical energy, such as lights, fans, televisions, refrigerators, microwave ovens, and computers. Wall switches control some of these devices. Others have their own built-in switches. In addition, there are wires in a home that supply the electric current needed to run these devices. These wires are typically hidden from view and are often part of a larger circuit with many side branches.

In this lab, you will build a model of a room wired to supply electrical energy from a battery to three different appliances. Your model will include switches that you can use to control the appliances. Before you build your model, you will develop a plan by drawing an electric circuit to simulate your model room with its three appliances and their switches. You will then check the feasibility of your circuit by building the model and testing it.

OBJECTIVES

- Draw an electric circuit that models the lights and appliances in a room.
- Test the circuit by building a model using wire, batteries, and light bulbs.

MATERIALS

- batteries, Type D, with holders (2)
- light bulbs, small, with holders (3)
- paper
- shoe box
- switches (3)
- tape, electrical
- tape, transparent
- wire cutter
- wire, insulated

For each student

- lab apron
- safety goggles

PROCEDURE

ASK A QUESTION

1 You will build a model that meets the following criteria:

- The circuit must model one room of a house that includes a ceiling light and two "appliances."
- Each light or appliance must be on a different wall of the room.
- Each part of the circuit must be activated by a separate switch.
- The circuit must work according to a diagram that you prepare before you build the physical model.

In order to take the first step toward building your model, consider the following question: Before an electrician wires a circuit for a room in a house, what does the electrician do to plan the circuit to be constructed?

____

____

____

Name ______________________ Class ______________ Date ______________

Exploration Lab continued

DEVELOP A PLAN

2 Would a series circuit or a parallel circuit work better for your room model? Explain.

____

____

____

3 A circuit diagram uses symbols to represent the components of the circuit. Because light bulbs are the only devices available, you will use them as stand-ins for “appliances” in your working model. How will you represent the “appliances” in.your circuit diagram?

____

4 Work with the other members of your group to draw a circuit diagram on the paper provided. Use the electrical symbol key shown below to represent parts of the circuit diagram as you plan your room.

Electric symbol key	
Wire	
Crossed wire (not connected)	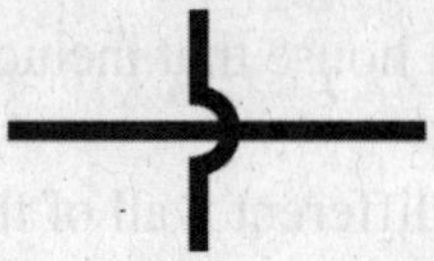
Battery	
Lamp	
Switch	

Exploration Lab continued

BUILD A MODEL

5 In most homes, the source of electrical energy is outside the home. How could your model represent this?

____

6 Use the provided materials to build a physical model of your room based on the circuit diagram you drew in Step 4.

ANALYZE THE RESULTS

7 **Developing Models** Test your design by connecting the batteries. If necessary, change your circuit until it works correctly. If you change your circuit, make the same changes on your circuit diagram.

DRAW CONCLUSIONS

8 **Describing Results** Did your circuit work as expected?

____

____

____

9 **Evaluating Models** Did you have to make any changes to the design of your circuit? Explain.

____

____

____

Connect TO THE ESSENTIAL QUESTION

10 **Explaining Observations** With all switches open, none of the appliances work. What happens when you close each switch? Explain.

____

____

____

QUICK LAB DIRECTED Inquiry

Making Magnets GENERAL

Student pairs
20 minutes

MATERIALS

For each pair

- bowl
- foam squares 2 cm × 2 cm (6)
- magnet, bar
- needle, sewing (6)
- paper towel
- water

For each student

- lab apron
- safety goggles

LAB RATINGS

LESS ⟷ MORE

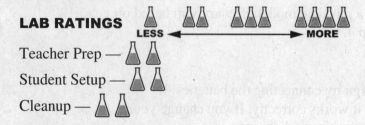

Teacher Prep — 2
Student Setup — 2
Cleanup — 2

SAFETY INFORMATION

Remind students to review all safety cautions and icons before beginning this lab. Tell students to be careful when handling the needles because they are very sharp. Demonstrate how to push the needle through the foam square, emphasizing that is must be done slowly and carefully. Be sure students do not attempt to push the needle with their bare hands. Instruct them to wrap a small piece of paper towel around the opposite end of the needle before they push the sharp end through the foam square. Also, instruct students to fill their bowls only halfway to reduce the chance of spills. Immediately wipe up any spilled water.

My Notes

TEACHER NOTES

In this activity, students will observe that a steel sewing needle is not naturally magnetized but can become magnetized when a bar magnet is rubbed along its length. Students will also explore the properties of magnetic fields by observing how a bar magnet attracts or repels a set of magnetized needles depending on which pole of the bar magnet is held close to the needles.

The foam material used to make squares can be purchased in a hobby store or the crafts section of a discount department store. Cut small squares of foam ahead of class time. Warn students that they need to take care to keep the bar magnet away from needles except when they are using it to rub them. Note that needles will float if the eye of the needle is pointing up or if it is down in the water. If a student rubs one needle in the direction toward the eye rather than toward the point as directed, he or she can simply flip the orientation of the needle in the water to make all the poles consistent within that group of needles.

Tip This activity will help students understand induction of magnetism and magnetic fields.

Skills Focus Making Observations, Explaining Concepts

MODIFICATION FOR INDEPENDENT Inquiry

Have students follow the directions from Steps 1–6. Then ask students to use the available materials to devise a way to demonstrate that magnets have poles. Allow students to freely experiment with needles, foam squares, water, and the bar magnet; ask students to record their procedure and observations as they experiment. Circulate around the room, providing suggestions to students struggling to come up with reasonable experiments.

Quick Lab continued

Answer Key

1. Sample answer: No, the first needle just sits there without moving.

4. Sample answer: The first needle jumped from the table and stuck to the one I was holding.

5. Sample answer: The needles were not magnetized before I rubbed them with the bar magnet. They became magnetized when I rubbed them with the bar magnet. This caused them to become attracted to each other.
Teacher Prompt What happened that caused the needles to be attracted to one another?

9. Answers will vary depending on which pole of the bar magnet is lowered (i.e., One pole will attract the needles, which will cause the needles to move to the center of the bowl. The other pole will repel the needles, which will cause the needles to move to the perimeter of the bowl).

10. Answers will vary depending on which pole of the bar magnet is lowered. Be sure that students' answers to 9 and 10 are opposite.

11. Answers will vary depending on which pole of the bar magnet is lowered. Students should observe that the needles are attracted to one pole of the bar magnet but repelled by the other.

12. Sample answer: When the needles were magnetized, they developed poles. We could see this because their poles were attracted to one pole of the bar magnet and repelled by the other pole of the bar magnet.

13. Sample answer: The bar magnet didn't have to touch any of the needles. The magnetic force acted without the bar magnet coming into contact with any of the needles.

Name ______________________ Class ______________ Date ________________

QUICK LAB DIRECTED *Inquiry*

Making Magnets

In this lab, you will explore the properties of magnetized needles to learn more about magnetic fields and magnetic poles.

OBJECTIVES

- Use a permanent magnet to magnetize an iron-containing material.
- Observe how the magnetized objects interact with each other.
- Observe how the magnetized objects interact with the permanent magnet.

MATERIALS

For each pair of students

- bowl
- foam squares 2 cm × 2 cm (6)
- magnet, bar
- needle, sewing (6)
- paper towel
- water

For each student

- lab apron
- safety goggles

PROCEDURE

1. Take one sewing needle and place it on a flat surface. Take a second needle and bring it close to the first one without touching it. Does the first needle move?

   ____

   ____

2. Hold the eye of one needle between your fingers. Rub one pole of the bar magnet along the needle, from one end of the needle to the other. Lift up the magnet and repeat. Do this about 25 times, rubbing in the same direction each time. Place the needle far away from your setup.

3. Repeat Step 2 with the second needle. Now place the bar magnet far away from your setup.

4. Place the needle from Step 3 on a flat surface. Bring the needle from Step 2 close to it. What do you observe?

   ____

   ____

5. Explain why the needle behavior changed.

   ____

   ____

   ____

6. Fill the bowl about halfway with water.

Name ______________________________Class ________________ Date ______________________

Quick Lab continued

7. Rub a needle with the bar magnet as you did in Step 2. Wrap a small piece of paper towel around the tip of the needle opposite the pointed end. Carefully and slowly push the needle through the middle of a 2 centimeter (cm) × 2 cm foam square. Place this on the water so that the foam square floats with the eye of the needle pointing up.

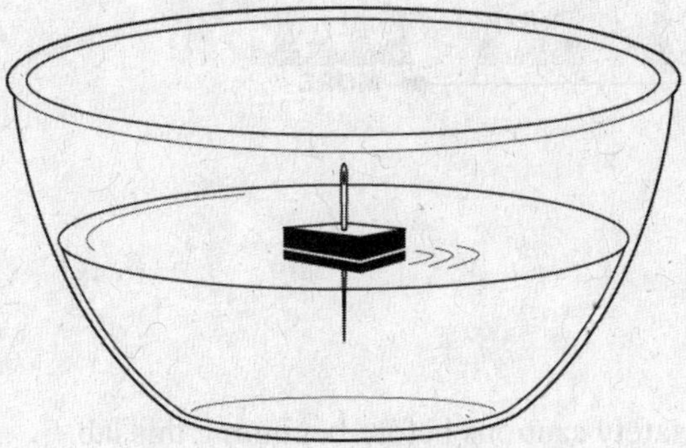

8. Repeat Step 7 five times so that you have six needles floating vertically on the water.

9. Carefully position the bar magnet about 30 cm above the bowl of water so that one end of the magnet is directed downward. Slowly lower the bar magnet and observe any changes in the needles. What do you observe as the bar magnet gets closer to the needles?

____

____

10. What do you predict will happen if you repeat Step 9 but use the opposite pole of the bar magnet to bring it closer to the needles?

____

____

11. Test your prediction. Write your observations below.

____

____

12. How does this activity demonstrate that magnets have poles?

____

____

13. How does this activity demonstrate that magnets exert their magnetic force through an invisible field?

____

____

QUICK LAB DIRECTED *Inquiry*

Studying Magnetism GENERAL

Small groups
20 minutes

LAB RATINGS

LESS ⟵ ⟶ MORE

Teacher Prep —
Student Setup —
Cleanup —

SAFETY INFORMATION

Remind students to review all safety cautions before beginning this lab.

TEACHER NOTES

In this activity, students will investigate two variables to see how they affect the strength of attraction between a magnet and a metal object. The two variables are: 1) distance between magnet and object, and 2) type of barrier placed between magnet and object. Note that no material blocks magnetic fields, but some materials can re-route them. For example, re-routing is responsible for the magnetic shielding around MRIs.

Warn students that air breezes caused by excessive movement in the classroom can disturb others' attempts to keep their paper clip still.

Tip This activity may help students understand that magnetic forces decrease with distance, and that magnetic fields are not blocked by physical barriers.

Skills Focus Making Observations, Drawing Conclusions

MODIFICATION FOR GUIDED *Inquiry*

Show students how you can move a magnet along the surface of a table toward a metal object. At some point, the metal object will jump toward, and stick to, the magnet. Then ask them to plan an experiment to measure this distance. Allow students to develop their own procedure and to obtain your approval before they begin. After they have run their tests, ask them to explore the effects of placing various physical barriers of their choice in between the magnet and the object.

MATERIALS

For each group

- aluminum foil
- board, wood
- cardboard
- cloth
- magnet, bar
- paper
- paper clip
- ruler, metric
- tape
- thread (80 cm length)

My Notes

Quick Lab continued

Answer Key

3. Answers will vary.
4. Sample answer: The paper clip moved toward the magnet because the magnetic field of the magnet came close enough to cause attraction. Or, the paper clip moved away from the magnet because the magnetic field of the magnet came close enough to cause repulsion.
5. Answers will vary.
6. Answers will vary.
7. Answers will vary.
8. Sample answer: The magnet's force is not affected by wood, cloth, or aluminum foil. Physical barriers don't block magnetic force.
9. Sample answer: It was hard to know exactly when to stop moving the magnet toward the paper clip. This made the distances slightly different between trials, so we had to run several trials to get a better idea of each distance we should be seeing.

Name ______________________________ Class ____________________ Date ______________________

QUICK LAB DIRECTED Inquiry

Studying Magnetism

In your own experience, you have likely wondered what causes an object to be attracted to a magnet. You may also have wondered whether that attractive force is affected by distance and whether a barrier placed between the object and the magnet might block the magnetic force of attraction. In this lab, you will explore these questions to learn more about magnetism.

OBJECTIVES

- Investigate the ability of a magnet to attract or repel a metal object as distance is varied between magnet and object.
- Investigate the ability of a magnet to attract or repel a metal object when various materials are placed between the magnet and the object.

MATERIALS

For each group

- aluminum foil
- board, wood
- cardboard
- cloth
- magnet, bar
- paper
- paper clip
- ruler, metric
- tape
- thread (80 cm length)

PROCEDURE

1. Tie one end of the thread to the paper clip. Dangle the paper clip from the thread next to a table or desk so that it is suspended about 1 centimeter (cm) from the floor. Tape the top end of the thread to the desk. The paper clip should be able to move freely.

2. Mark an X on a sheet of paper. Slide the paper under the paper clip so that when at rest, the paper clip is directly over the X on the paper.

3. Place the bar magnet on the floor and slowly slide the magnet toward the paper clip. Stop sliding the magnet when you observe that the paper clip moves from its resting position over the X on the paper. Record that distance below. Repeat this two more times, recording your results each time.

____

____

____

4. Which way did the paper clip move in each of your trials above? What force caused the movement?

____

____

5. Test whether a physical barrier can block the magnetic force of attraction. Repeat your experiment from Step 3 but place a block of wood in between the magnet and the paper clip. Record your data below. Run at least three trials.

____

____

____

Quick Lab continued

6 Repeat Step 5 using cloth as a barrier. Record your data below.

____

____

____

7 Repeat Step 5 using aluminum foil as a barrier. Record your data below.

____

____

____

8 What conclusion do you draw about the ability of a magnet to attract or repel a metal object when any of the barriers you tried are placed in between the magnet and the object?

____

____

9 Why was it necessary to run multiple trials in each of the steps above?

____

____

____

QUICK LAB DIRECTED Inquiry

Building an Electromagnet BASIC

Student pairs

15 minutes

LAB RATINGS

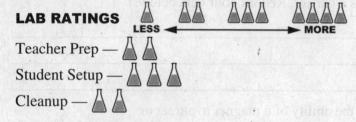

LESS ← → MORE

Teacher Prep — 2 flasks

Student Setup — 3 flasks

Cleanup — 2 flasks

MATERIALS

For each pair

- batteries, D-cell (2)
- nail, iron, 3 1/2 in.
- paper clip
- scissors
- tape, electrical
- wire, enameled (magnet)

For each student

- safety goggles

SAFETY INFORMATION

Remind students to review all safety cautions and icons before beginning this lab. Before class, check all batteries to be sure they are working. A battery's strength is known by the amperage it produces, not by its voltage; amperage must be measured by an amp meter or multimeter.

My Notes

TEACHER NOTES

In this activity, students will build an electromagnet and observe how it works. Before class, you might want to cut the lengths of wire required to complete the lab. To determine the length of wire needed for each group, wrap the wire around a nail completely, unwrap it, and add about 50 centimeters (cm) to the length used to wrap the nail. Use a wire stripper to remove about 1 cm of insulation from each end of each length of wire. Test the paper clips to make sure they are not aluminum.

Tip This activity will help students understand that an electric current can produce a magnetic field.

Student Tip Think about why the wire-wrapped nail cannot pick up the paper clip when the wire is not attached to the batteries.

Skills Focus Making Observations, Drawing Conclusions

MODIFICATION FOR INDEPENDENT Inquiry

Challenge students to build an electromagnet that can pick up at least three paper clips. Ask students to devise a plan to meet this challenge, and provide them with a list of materials. After you have checked their plans, allow them to collect their materials and proceed. Remind students to record every step of their process. Last, ask students to draw a diagram of their functional electromagnet and to write a paragraph summarizing their process.

Quick Lab continued

Answer Key

3. Accept all reasonable answers. Sample answer: The paper clip stayed on the table.
Teacher Prompt Did the paper clip move?

4. Accept all reasonable answers. Sample answer: The paper clip stuck to the tip of the nail.
Teacher Prompt What happened to the paper clip?

5. Accept all reasonable answers. Sample answer: The paper clip will fall to the table.
Teacher Prompt What caused the difference that you observed between Step 3 and Step 4?

6. Sample answer: The paper clip fell from the nail when the wire was disconnected. When I disconnected the wire, there was no electric current in the wire, so the electromagnet no longer had a magnetic field.
Teacher Prompt What is the difference between a closed circuit and an open circuit?

Name ______________________ Class ______________ Date ______________

QUICK LAB

Building an Electromagnet

In this lab, you will build an electromagnet. An electromagnet is a device that produces a magnetic field from an electric current.

OBJECTIVES

- Build an electromagnet.
- Observe how an electromagnet works.

MATERIALS

For each pair

- batteries, D-cell (2)
- nail, iron, 3 1/2 in.
- paper clip
- scissors
- tape, electrical
- wire, enameled (magnet)

For each student

- safety goggles

PROCEDURE

1. Starting about 25 centimeters (cm) from one end of the wire, wrap the wire in tight coils around the nail. The coils should cover the nail from the head almost to the point.
2. Use the electrical tape to fasten the two batteries together. Tape one end of the wire to a free battery terminal.

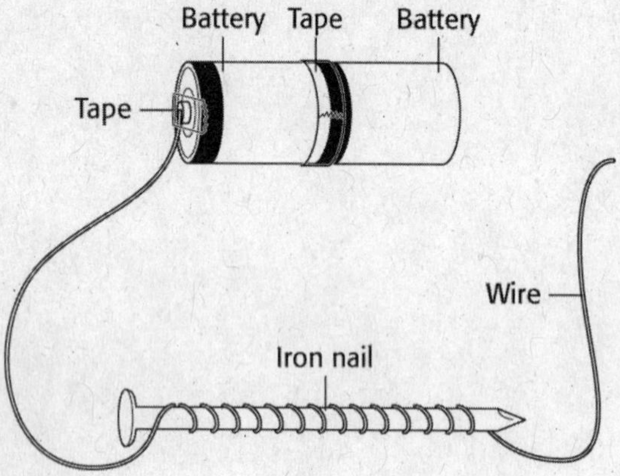

3. Touch the point of the nail to a paper clip and record your observations.

____

4. Connect the other end of the wire to the other battery terminal as you did in Step 2. Again, touch the point of the nail to a paper clip. Record your observations.

____

____

____

____

____

____

____

____

Quick Lab continued

5 Predict what will happen if you disconnect the wire from the battery.

____

____

____

____

____

____

6 Disconnect the wire. Explain your observations.

____

____

____

____

____

QUICK LAB DIRECTED Inquiry

Making an Electric Generator GENERAL

Small groups
25 minutes

LAB RATINGS LESS ⟷ MORE

Teacher Prep — 2
Student Setup — 2
Cleanup — 1

MATERIALS

For each group
- cardboard tubes, 1 narrow and 1 wide
- coated magnet wire, 16 meters
- galvanometer
- magnet, strong
- scissors

For each student
- safety goggles

My Notes

SAFETY INFORMATION

Remind students to review all safety cautions and icons before beginning this lab. Use caution when using the scissors to strip plastic from the wire. Press the wire into a desk or other work surface, not hands, when stripping the plastic coating.

TEACHER NOTES

In this activity, students will construct a simple generator. They will use wires and a magnet to explore how an electric current is induced by a changing magnetic field. A galvanometer is needed. To make a simple galvanometer, wrap 20 turns of wire around a magnetic compass, leaving about 10 cm of stripped wire at each end. Empty paper towel or toilet paper rolls can be used for cardboard tubes. Paper towel rolls should be cut in half so they are not too long for the magnet to penetrate. To remove the plastic coating from the wire, scrape a scissor blade along the wire while pressing firmly.

Tip Remind students to wrap the wide tube first; otherwise, they will not have enough wire.

Student Tip Strip the plastic coating off only the very ends of the wire.

Skills Focus Making Observations, Drawing Conclusions, Designing Technology

MODIFICATION FOR GUIDED Inquiry

Rather than using a galvanometer, have students use their generators to power a tiny light bulb. A 1.5 watt bulb will work. Students should create a procedure for their experiment, including how the bulb attaches to the generator. With approval, students should carry out their procedures. They may need to modify and repeat their experiments until they achieve the desired results.

Quick Lab continued

Answer Key

4. Sample answer: When the magnet moves through the coils, the needle on the galvanometer moves.

5. Sample answer: The faster the magnet moves, the farther the needle on the galvanometer moves.

6. Sample answer: The needle deflects in the opposite direction first.

7. Sample answer: The smaller the coils, the more the galvanometer deflects.

8. Sample answer: Electric current flows through the coils.
Teacher Prompt The needle of a galvanometer experiences a force when an electric current is present.

9. Sample answer: I would make a generator with very small coils, and I would move the magnet very quickly through them.
Teacher Prompt When did the galvanometer deflect the most? Think about the size of the coils and the speed of the magnet.

Name ______________________ Class ______________ Date ______________

QUICK LAB DIRECTED *Inquiry*

Making an Electric Generator

In this lab, you will construct an electric generator. A generator is a machine that converts kinetic energy into electricity. You will use magnets and wire to generate electricity.

OBJECTIVES

- Construct an electric generator.
- Investigate electrical energy.

MATERIALS

For each group

- cardboard tubes, 1 narrow and 1 wide
- coated magnet wire, 16 meters
- galvanometer
- magnet, strong
- scissors

For each student

- safety goggles

PROCEDURE

1. Carefully wrap 100 turns of coated wire around a wide **cardboard tube**.
2. Using **scissors**, carefully strip insulation from the ends of the wires, baring about 3 cm of wire.
3. Connect the ends of the wire to the wires on the **galvanometer** by twisting them together.
4. With a quick motion, move the **magnet** into the tube and observe the galvanometer. Make sure the magnet is deep enough to enter the loop of wire. Then, pull the magnet out of the tube. Watch the galvanometer and record your observations.

____

____

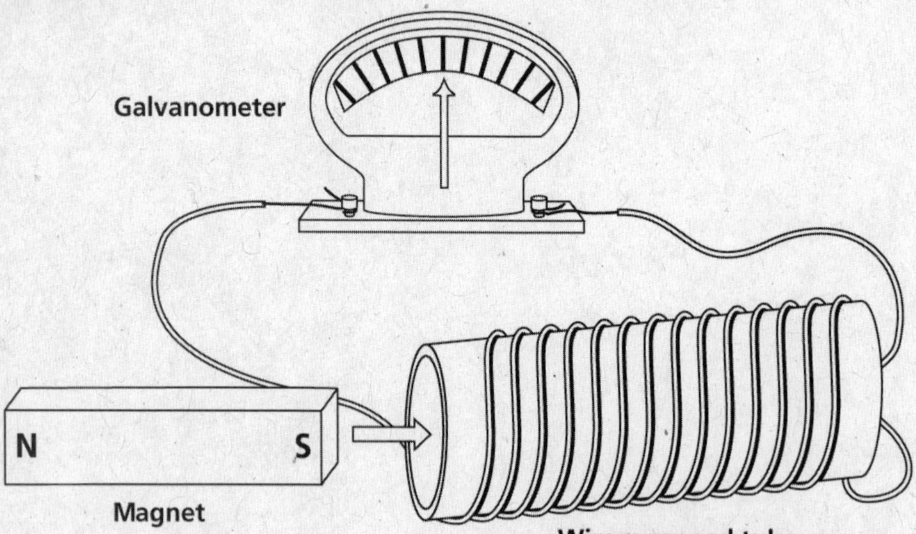

5. Try different speeds by inserting the magnet faster and slower. What do you notice?

6. Try a different magnetic orientation by inserting the magnet the opposite way. What do you notice?

7. Repeat the investigation for the **narrow cardboard tube**. How does the size of the coils change the reading on the galvanometer?

8. Based on your observations, what happens in the wire when you move the magnet through the coils?

9. If you wanted to create a powerful generator, how would you construct the coils and the magnet?

S.T.E.M. LAB GUIDED Inquiry AND INDEPENDENT Inquiry

Building a Speaker ADVANCED

Small groups
45 minutes

LAB RATINGS

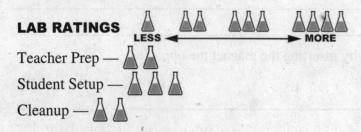

LESS ⟷ MORE

Teacher Prep — 2
Student Setup — 3
Cleanup — 2

MATERIALS

For each group

- cable, 1/8 in. input
- cup, plastic
- magnets, disc, 3 different strengths (3)
- paper clip
- pencil
- radio (or mp3 player with headphone output)
- ruler, metric
- tape, masking
- wire, enameled (magnet), ends stripped (2 m)
- wire, insulated with alligator clips (2)

For each student

- safety goggles

SAFETY INFORMATION

Remind students to review all safety cautions and icons before beginning this lab. Be sure that students turn the radio off when connecting (or disconnecting) the electromagnet wire ends to (or from) the eighth-inch cord. Remind students that they should not adjust the radio volume too high, because this can cause hearing damage.

TEACHER NOTES

In this activity, students will investigate variables that affect the volume of sound produced by an electromagnet speaker. The following factors may affect sound volume: magnet strength, number of turns in the wire coil, height of the coil in relation to the magnet, and audio device used as the sound source. Students can use a radio, mp3 player, or other sound device with a headphone output as the source for their sound. One radio can be shared by the entire class. To prepare the sound source, obtain an eighth-inch cable that can be plugged into the radio's headphone output. Then, cut this so that the two leads inside the cable are exposed. Students will be connecting the ends of their electromagnet wires to these leads. For best results, have students use 22-gauge magnet wire to form their electromagnet coils. Results may be poor if using wire with a gauge below AWG 32.You can strip the ends of the wire using a wire stripper or by scraping them with sandpaper, or you may use pre-stripped wire.

Tip It is advisable that students perform this activity in a quiet area so that they can best observe the volume of sound produced by the speaker. You may consider turning off any heaters or air-conditioners to reduce the ambient noise in the classroom.

Student Tip If the coils of wire do not stay in place on the bottom of the cup, you may wrap the loose ends of the wire around the stack of coils once to secure them to each other. Also, be careful not to touch the cup during your experiment—interfering with the vibrations of the cup will affect the sound produced.

Skills Focus Devising Procedures, Identifying Variables, Making Observations

My Notes

___

___

___

___

___

S.T.E.M. Lab continued

MODIFICATION FOR DIRECTED Inquiry

Have students set up the electromagnet following the procedure detailed in the student datasheets. Tell them that they will be investigating how the strength of the permanent magnet affects the volume of the sound produced by the speaker. Have the students determine the strength of each magnet by placing a paper clip near the magnet and observing the distance that the paper clip is displaced by the magnetic force. Direct students to record this distance in a chart on their datasheets.

To investigate how the magnet strength affects the volume of sound produced, advise students to move the speaker assembly close to a magnet and observe the volume of sound produced. Have them repeat this process for each of the remaining magnets. Students should then analyze the results to determine a relationship between magnet strength and sound volume.

Answer Key For GUIDED Inquiry

MAKE OBSERVATIONS

5. Accept all reasonable answers.

FORM A PREDICTION

7. Accept all reasonable answers.

DEVELOP A PLAN

8. Accept all reasonable answers.
Teacher Prompt To determine the strength of each magnet, think about what strong magnets do. How do strong magnets interact with metallic objects, such as paper clips? How would a weak magnet interact with a paper clip? How could you use a paper clip to determine the strength of a permanent magnet?

EVALUATE THE PLAN

10. Answers will vary.

ANALYZE THE RESULTS

11. The cup is the diaphragm of this speaker.

12. Sample answer: As the magnet strength increased, the volume of the speaker increased.

DRAW CONCLUSIONS

13. Answers will vary.

14. Sample answer: The speaker assembly turns into an electromagnet when the radio is turned on and an electric current is in the coils of wire attached to the cup.
Teacher Prompt Remember that magnetic fields are produced when electric current is in a wire.

S.T.E.M. Lab continued

15. Sample answer: The speaker assembly must be moved close to the permanent magnet so that the magnetic field from the permanent magnet will interact with the magnetic field produced by the electromagnet.
Teacher Prompt What are some properties of magnets? What happens when you move magnets close to one another? What happens when you move them apart? Remember that the speaker assembly has a magnetic field when the electric current from the radio is in the coiled wire on the cup.

16. Sample answer: The strength of the permanent magnet determines how forcefully the magnet and speaker assembly will attract and repel each other. The more forceful the interaction, the more the speaker will vibrate. If the speaker vibrates more intensely, the volume of sound will be greater.
Teacher Prompt Think about how the stronger permanent magnet interacts with the paper clip. Then, think about how the permanent magnet interacts with the electromagnet on the bottom of the cup. Remember that sound is produced by vibrating materials. The larger the vibration, the louder the sound.

Connect TO THE ESSENTIAL QUESTIONS

17. Sample answer: The electromagnet we made takes electrical energy and converts this to mechanical energy in the form of vibrations, which produces the sound we hear. By varying position or strength of the magnet, the volume of sound can be varied.

Answer Key For INDEPENDENT Inquiry

MAKE OBSERVATIONS

5. Accept all reasonable answers.

ASK A QUESTION

6. Accept all reasonable answers.
Teacher Prompt Think about the different things that might cause sound to emit from the speaker. Think about the role of the permanent magnet. Do you think the speaker would work without it? How might the properties of this magnet affect the sound produced by the speaker?

FORM A PREDICTION

7. Accept all reasonable answers.

DEVELOP A PLAN

8. Accept all reasonable steps.
Teacher Prompt Think about how you will change your chosen variable. Think about how you will measure and record the volume of the speaker after each trial.

EVALUATE THE PLAN

10. Answers will vary.

S.T.E.M. Lab continued

ANALYZE THE RESULTS

11. The cup is the diaphragm of this speaker.

12. Sample answer: As the magnet strength increased, the volume of the speaker increased.

DRAW CONCLUSIONS

13. Answers will vary.

14. Sample answer: The speaker assembly turns into an electromagnet when the radio is turned on and an electric current is in the coils of wire attached to the cup.
Teacher Prompt Remember that magnetic fields are produced when electric current is in a wire.

15. Sample answer: The speaker assembly must be moved close to the permanent magnet so that the magnetic field from the permanent magnet will interact with the magnetic field produced by the electromagnet.
Teacher Prompt What are some properties of magnets? What happens when you move magnets close to one another? What happens when you move them apart? Remember that the speaker assembly has a magnetic field when the electric current from the radio is in the coiled wire on the cup.

16. Answers will vary, but students should demonstrate that they drew correct conclusions based on results obtained as they varied their chosen variable.

17. Answers will vary, but students should demonstrate that they identified a different variable that could be tested and that they can describe a feasible method for conducting their test.

Connect TO THE ESSENTIAL QUESTIONS

18. Sample answer: The electromagnet we made takes electrical energy and converts this to mechanical energy in the form of vibrations, which produces the sound we hear. By varying position or strength of the magnet, the volume of sound can be varied.

Name ______________________________ Class ________________ Date ______________________

S.T.E.M LAB GUIDED *Inquiry*

Building a Speaker

In this lab, you will investigate a variable that affects the volume of an electromagnet speaker. Remember that when an electric current is in a wire, magnetic fields will form around the wire. This creates an electromagnet. If you run a signal from a source such as a radio through loops of wire, you will create an electromagnet with properties that alter very quickly because of the changes in the signal. When you place this electromagnet near a permanent magnet, the magnets will attract and repel each other very quickly, causing the magnets to vibrate. This vibration will produce sound that you can hear!

OBJECTIVES

- Describe the relationship between electricity and magnetism, and how this relationship affects our world.
- Describe what an electromagnet is and how one is constructed.
- Describe some ways in which electromagnets are used in everyday life.

MATERIALS

For each group
- cable, 1/8 in. input
- cup, plastic
- magnets, disc, 3 different strengths (3)
- paper clip
- pencil
- radio (or mp3 player with headphone output)
- ruler, metric
- tape, masking
- wire, enameled (magnet), ends stripped (2 m)
- wire, insulated with alligator clips (2)

For each student
- safety goggles

PROCEDURE

MAKE OBSERVATIONS

1. Use your metric ruler to measure 6 centimeters (cm) from each end of the wire. Mark this point with an indelible marker. Starting at the 6 cm mark, wrap the insulated copper wire around the pencil 50 times and stop wrapping 6 cm from the end of the wire, as shown here:

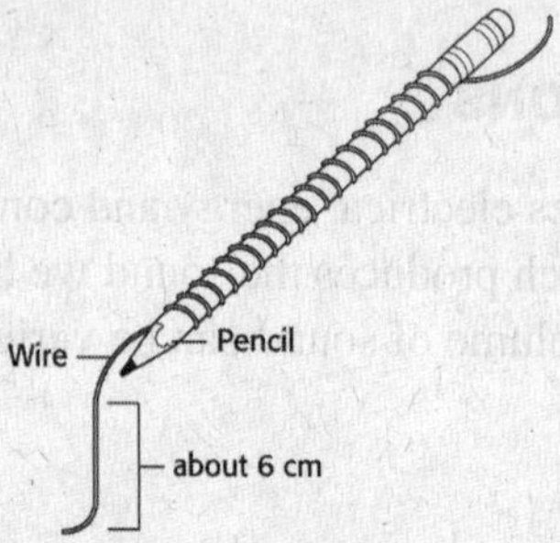

2. Carefully slide the coils of wire off the pencil. Turn the paper cup upside down and stack the coils onto the bottom of the cup. Tape them in place. Be sure to allow the ends of the coiled wire to hang off the side of the cup, as shown:

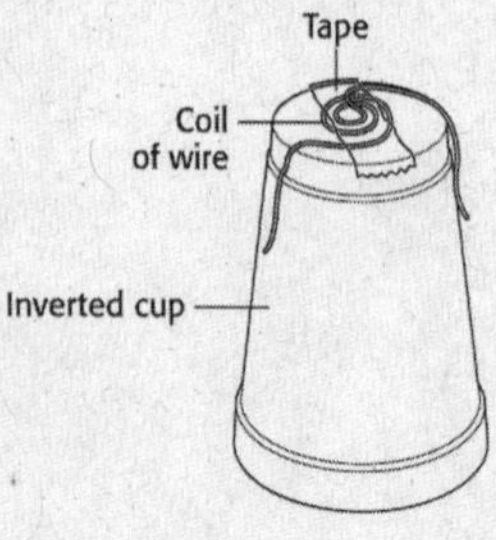

S.T.E.M. Lab continued

❸ Connect the wires with alligator clips to the loose ends of the coiled wire.

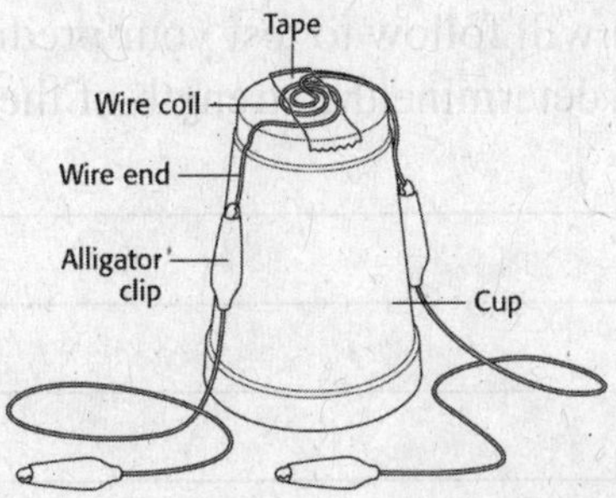

❹ Connect the loose alligator clips to the leads from the radio. Then, move the bottom of the cup near a permanent magnet, as shown:

❺ Turn on the radio, and slowly turn up the volume. Place your ear toward the opening of the cup and listen. What are your observations?

____

____

____

ASK A QUESTION

❻ Think about how the strength of a permanent magnet might affect the loudness of the music emitting from the speaker.

FORM A PREDICTION

❼ Predict how the strength of the permanent magnet will affect the volume of the speaker.

____

____

____

Name ______________________ Class ______________ Date ______________

S.T.E.M. Lab continued

DEVELOP A PLAN

8. Write a list of steps that you will follow to test your prediction. (Be sure to include steps that you will follow to determine the strength of the permanent magnet.)

9. Carry out the investigation. Be sure to record all your observations.

EVALUATE THE PLAN

10. Analyze the procedure that you followed. Did you encounter any problems while collecting data? If so, describe how you would change the procedure to eliminate those problems.

ANALYZE THE RESULTS

11. **Analyzing Models** The diaphragm on a speaker vibrates to produce sound. Which part of your speaker is the diaphragm?

12. **Examining Data** What happened to the volume of the music coming out of the speaker as the strength of the permanent magnet increased?

DRAW CONCLUSIONS

13. **Evaluating Predictions** Did your observations in this investigation support your prediction?

14. **Applying Concepts** What causes the speaker assembly to turn into an electromagnet?

15. **Explaining Methods** Explain why you needed to move the speaker assembly close to the permanent magnet to hear a sound.

S.T.E.M. Lab continued

16 **Interpreting Observations** Why do you think the strength of the permanent magnet affects the volume of the sound produced by the speaker?

____

____

Connect TO THE ESSENTIAL QUESTION

17 **Identifying Concepts** How do the results of this lab demonstrate how sound is produced and modified in a speaker?

____

____

____

____

____

____

Name ______________________ Class ______________ Date ______________________

S.T.E.M LAB INDEPENDENT Inquiry

Building a Speaker

In this lab, you will investigate a variable that affects the volume of an electromagnet speaker. Remember that when an electric current is in a wire, magnetic fields will form around the wire. This creates an electromagnet. If you run a signal from a source such as a radio through loops of wire, you will create an electromagnet with properties that alter very quickly because of the changes in the signal. When you place this electromagnet near a permanent magnet, the magnets will attract and repel each other very quickly, causing the magnets to vibrate. This vibration will produce sound that you can hear!

OBJECTIVES

- Describe the relationship between electricity and magnetism and how this relationship affects our world.
- Describe what an electromagnet is and how one is constructed.
- Describe some ways in which electromagnets are used in everyday life.

MATERIALS

For each group:

- cable, 1/8 in. input
- cup, plastic
- magnets, disc, 3 different strengths (3)
- paper clip
- pencil
- radio (or mp3 player with headphone output)
- ruler, metric
- tape, masking
- wire, enameled (magnet), ends stripped (2 m)
- wire, insulated with alligator clips (2)

For each student

- safety goggles

PROCEDURE

Make Observations

1. Use your metric ruler to measure 6 centimeters (cm) from each end of the wire. Make this point with an indelible marker. Starting at the 6 cm mark, wrap the insulated copper wire around the pencil 50 times and stop wrapping 6 cm from the end of the wire, as shown here:

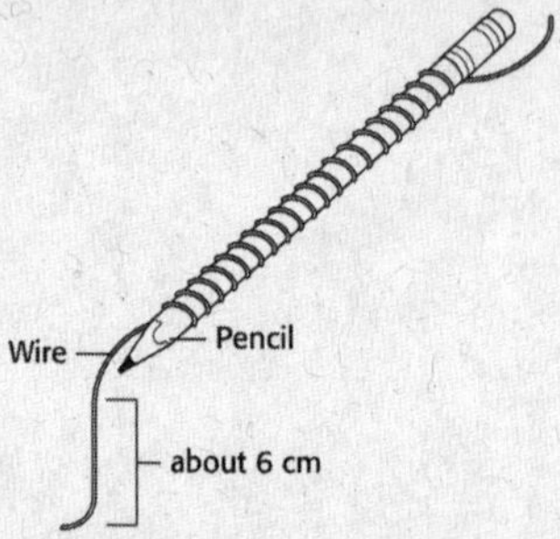

2. Carefully slide the coils of wire off the pencil. Turn the paper cup upside down and stack the coils onto the bottom of the cup. Tape them in place. Be sure to allow the ends of the coiled wire to hang off the side of the cup, as shown:

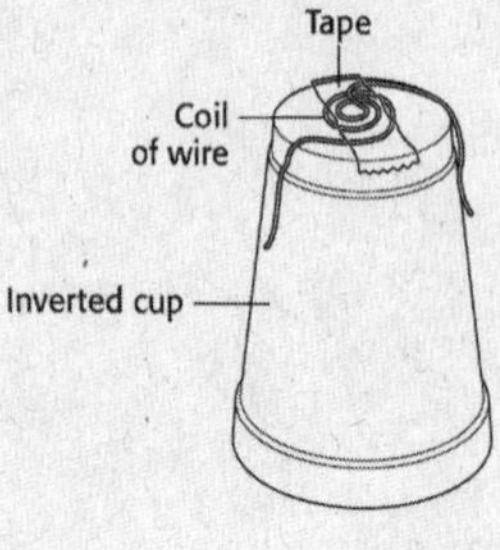

3. Connect the wires with alligator clips to the loose ends of the coiled wire, as shown:

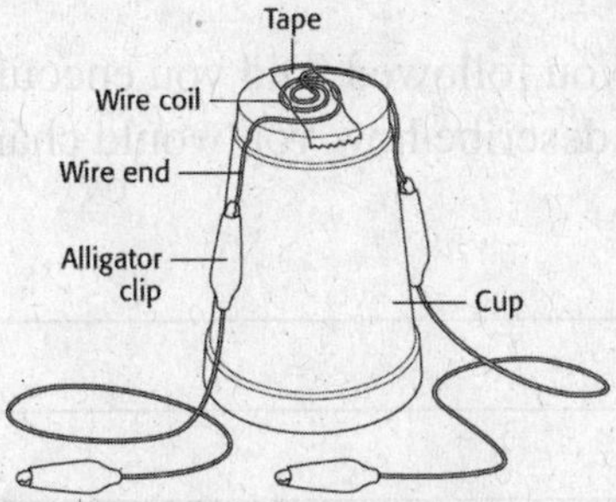

4. Connect the loose alligator clips to the leads from the radio. Then, move the bottom of the cup near a permanent magnet, as shown:

5. Turn on the radio and slowly turn up the volume. Place your ear toward the opening of the cup and listen. What are your observations?

____

ASK A QUESTION

6. What variable might affect the loudness of the music emitting from the speaker?

____

FORM A PREDICTION

7. Predict how the variable chosen in Step 6 will affect the volume of the speaker.

____

DEVELOP A PLAN

8. Write a list of steps that you will follow to test your prediction.

____

____

____

____

____

____

9 Carry out the investigation. Be sure to record all your observations.

EVALUATE THE PLAN

10 Analyze the procedure that you followed. Did you encounter any problems while collecting data? If so, describe how you would change the procedure to eliminate those problems.

____

____

____

ANALYZE THE RESULTS

11 **Analyzing Models** The diaphragm on a speaker vibrates to produce sound. Which part of your speaker is the diaphragm?

____

12 **Examining Data** What happened to the volume of the music coming out of the speaker as you modified your variable?

____

____

DRAW CONCLUSIONS

13 **Evaluating Predictions** Did your observations in this investigation support your prediction?

____

14 **Applying Concepts** What causes the speaker assembly to turn into an electromagnet?

____

____

15 **Explaining Methods** Explain why you needed to move the speaker assembly close to the permanent magnet to hear a sound.

____

____

____

S.T.E.M. Lab continued

16 **Interpreting Observations** Did the variable you chose to investigate affect the volume of the sound produced by the speaker? Explain why you think this was the case.

____

____

____

17 **Applying Methods** What other variables might affect the volume of the sound produced by the speaker? How could you test one of these variables?

____

____

____

____

____

____

Connect TO THE ESSENTIAL QUESTION

18 **Identifying Concepts** How do the results of this lab demonstrate how sound is produced and modified in a speaker?

____

____

____

____

____

____

____

____

____

____

____

____

____

____

____

QUICK LAB DIRECTED *Inquiry*

The Speed of a Simple Computer

GENERAL

Individual student
15 minutes

MATERIALS

For each group
- calculator
- clock, analog, with second hand (or stopwatch)

My Notes

LAB RATINGS

LESS ← → MORE

Teacher Prep —
Student Setup —
Cleanup —

TEACHER NOTES

In this activity, students will investigate the time it takes them to solve a series of math problems with and without a calculator. They will also compare accuracy rates for each method. Before the activity, prepare two problems sets, A and B, for students to complete. These problem sets should be equal in length and difficulty and appropriate for students' math skill level. For example, a problem set may consist of the following problems:

a. $(108 \div 9) + 231 - 19$
b. $1 \times 2 \times 3 \times 4 \times 5$
c. $(4 \times 6 \times 8) \div 2$
d. $3 \times (5 + 12) - 2$

Have students complete problem set A simultaneously, but instruct half the class to solve the problems using a calculator while the other half solves the problems without a calculator. Then, have students switch methods to complete problem set B. Students should check their answers for each problem set against an answer key. After students have completed both problem sets and recorded data, regroup as a class to calculate the average time and accuracy for each method (calculator versus no calculator) for each problem set.

Tip If necessary, review with students the order of operations before asking them to complete the problem sets.

Skills Focus Collecting Data, Drawing Conclusions

MODIFICATION FOR INDEPENDENT *Inquiry*

Have students design their own investigations to compare mathematical problem solving with and without calculators. Students may work in groups to devise procedures, identify variables, and create tables for data collection. Allow students to carry out their procedures and then compare results with other groups.

Quick Lab continued

6 What were the signals you used to send information? What was the carrier?

7 Were the signals digital or analog? How do you know?

8 Describe how binary code transmits information.

Name ______________________ Class ______________ Date ________________

QUICK LAB GUIDED *Inquiry*

Investigate Satellite Imaging

In this lab, you will use binary code to send or receive a color image. Satellites use a similar process to send images to Earth. To simulate the satellite imaging process, you will work in pairs; one of you will act as a "sensor," and the other will act as a "receiving station."

OBJECTIVES

- Identify how signals transmit information.
- Describe how binary code works.

MATERIALS

For each pair

- paper, graphing
- paper, plain
- pens or pencils, colored

PROCEDURE

1. With your partner, come up with a code for each of the different colored pencils or pens available to you. Each color should have a unique code using only the digits 1 and 0. Write your code keys below.

2. Choose one person to draw a color image in a 5 × 5 grid on a piece of graph paper. Do not show this image to your partner. Identify the digital code for each square.

3. With your partner, devise a procedure that will allow you to transmit the image using the code you created in Step 1. Carry out your procedure.

____

____

____

____

____

4. Have the partner acting as a receiving station use the code to reproduce the image on another piece of graph paper.

5. Was the picture reproduced accurately? If not, what were the sources of errors?

____

____

____

Quick Lab continued

Answer Key

1. Accept all reasonable answers.
3. Accept all reasonable answers.
5. Sample answer: One row was inaccurate because I skipped a square.
6. Sample answer: The signals were 1s and 0s. The carrier was the piece of paper that the signals were recorded on.
   Teacher prompt How was the information stored and transmitted? Did you use words, numbers, or something else? What carried the information?
7. The signals were digital because they were made up of only two values, 1 and 0.
   Teacher prompt What is the difference between digital and analog?
8. Binary code uses 1s and 0s to transmit information. Each digit is one binary digit, or bit. These digits can be arranged in different patterns to represent different information.
   Teacher prompt What values are possible in binary code? How can only two values transmit a wide variety of information?

QUICK LAB GUIDED *Inquiry*

Investigate Satellite Imaging GENERAL

Student pairs
15 minutes

MATERIALS

For each pair

- paper, graphing
- paper, plain
- pens or pencils, colored

LAB RATINGS LESS ◄—► MORE

Teacher Prep — 2
Student Setup — 1
Cleanup — 1

My Notes

TEACHER NOTES

In this activity, students will use binary code to transmit a color image to a partner. Students will decide on a code for each color using only the digits 1 and 0. Then they will determine how to transmit the coded image. For example, they may read the digital code aloud from left to right, top to bottom, or write the code on a piece of paper.

Tip To save time, you may give students images to transmit. A search for "free beginner cross-stitch patterns" will provide examples of how an image can be graphed.

Skills Focus Developing Models, Making Observations

MODIFICATION FOR DIRECTED *Inquiry*

Provide students with an image on a 5 x 5 grid and model how to record it in binary code. Then give students a procedure for transmitting their own color images. Have students write the binary code for their image on a piece of plain paper, beginning a new row of code for each new row of squares in the image. Students can then give the paper to a partner, who will reproduce the image.

Quick Lab continued

7. Does using a calculator guarantee that you will get the correct answer?

____

____

____

8. Is a calculator an electrical or an electronic device? Explain.

____

____

____

____

9. Is a calculator a simple computer? Why?

____

____

____

____

Name ______________________ Class ______________ Date ______________

QUICK LAB DIRECTED Inquiry

The Speed of a Simple Computer

In this lab, you will investigate how solving mathematical problems with a calculator compares to solving problems without a calculator. You will observe and record the speed and accuracy of each method and calculate class averages for each variable.

OBJECTIVE

- Compare human calculation speed and accuracy to those done by computer.

MATERIALS

For each student

- calculator
- clock, analog, with second hand (or stopwatch)

PROCEDURE

1. Obtain problem set A from your teacher. On your teacher's signal, solve the problem set using your assigned method (calculator or no calculator). Time this process using a clock or stopwatch.

2. Record data from problem set A below. Hint: To calculate the percentage of correct answers, divide the number of problems you solved correctly by the total number of problems and multiply the result by 100. It is acceptable to use a calculator to determine the percentage of correct answers.

Problem set	Method	Time	Percentage of answers correct
Problem Set A			
Problem Set B			

3. Obtain problem set B from your teacher. On your teacher's signal, solve the problem set using the method you did *not* use in Step 1.

4. Record data from problem set B in the table in Step 2.

5. As a class, calculate the average time needed for each method to complete each problem set. Also, calculate the average percentage of answers correct for each method. Record class averages below.

	With Calculator		Without Calculator	
Problem set	Average time	Average % correct	Average time	Average % correct
Problem Set A				
Problem Set B				

6. Which method was faster? Which method was more accurate?

____

____

Quick Lab continued

Answer Key

1. Accept all reasonable answers.
3. Accept all reasonable answers.
6. Using the calculator is faster, but it may or may not be more accurate.
7. Solving problems with a calculator does not guarantee that the answer will be correct. The person using the calculator must input the information correctly.
   Teacher Prompt Did you observe 100% accuracy for the calculator method? Why might results be less than 100% accurate?
8. A calculator is an electronic device because it can process information using integrated circuits.
   Teacher prompt A calculator has integrated circuits. How does this make it different from electrical devices, such as lamps?
9. Yes, it is a simple computer because it is an electronic device that performs tasks by following instructions given to it.
   Teacher prompt Is a calculator electronic? Does it follow instructions based on input?